SOME
WRITER!

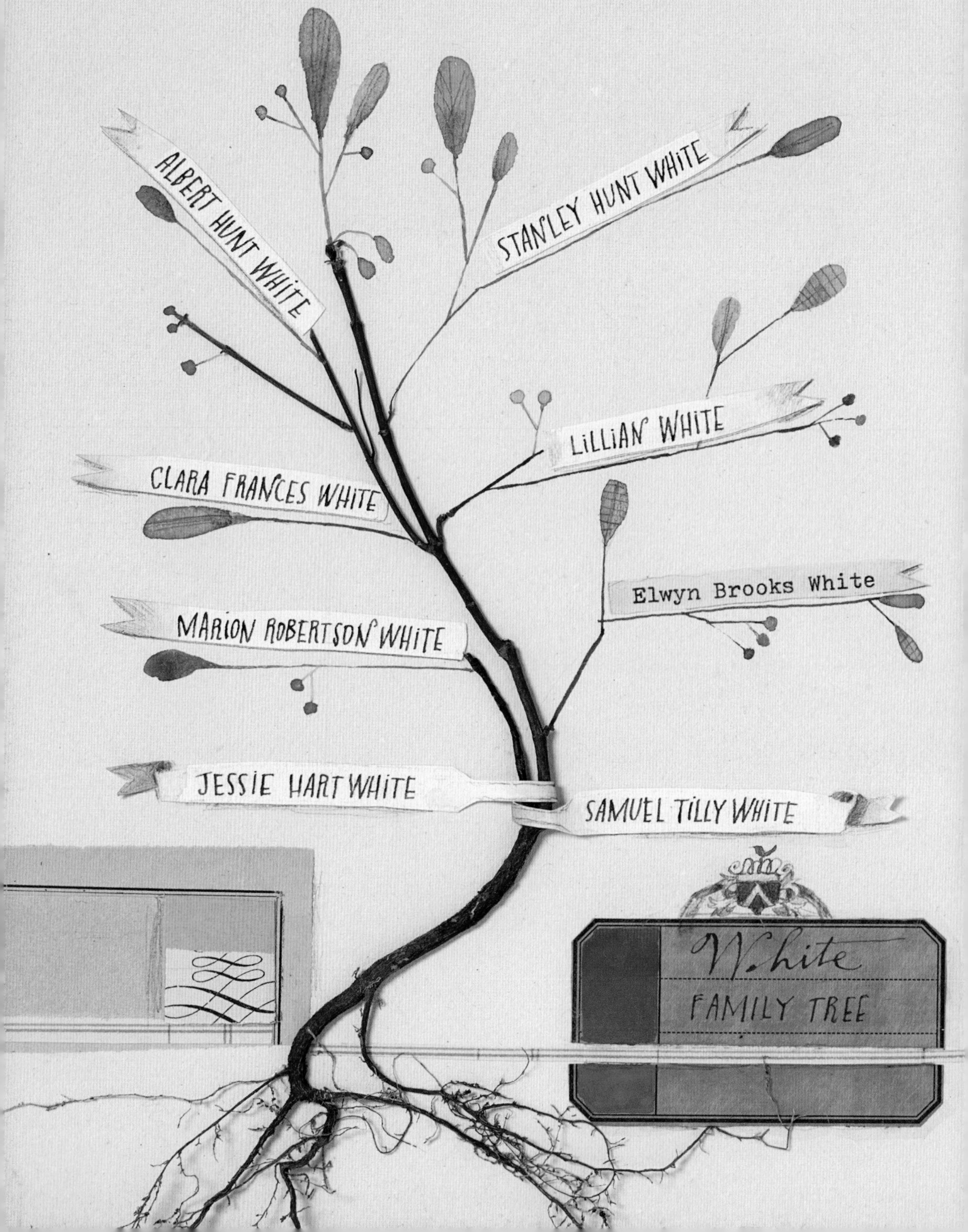

ALBERT HUNT WHITE

STANLEY HUNT WHITE

LILLIAN WHITE

CLARA FRANCES WHITE

Elwyn Brooks White

MARION ROBERTSON WHITE

JESSIE HART WHITE

SAMUEL TILLY WHITE

White
FAMILY TREE

1899

The White family from left to right:
Lillian, Samuel, Albert, Jessie, Elwyn, Stanley, Marion, Clara.

I BELIEVED THEN, as I do now, in the
goodness of the published word: it seemed
to contain an essential goodness, like
the smell of leaf mold.

—E. B. White

Elwyn, and the family dog Beppo, at his home in Mount Vernon, New York.

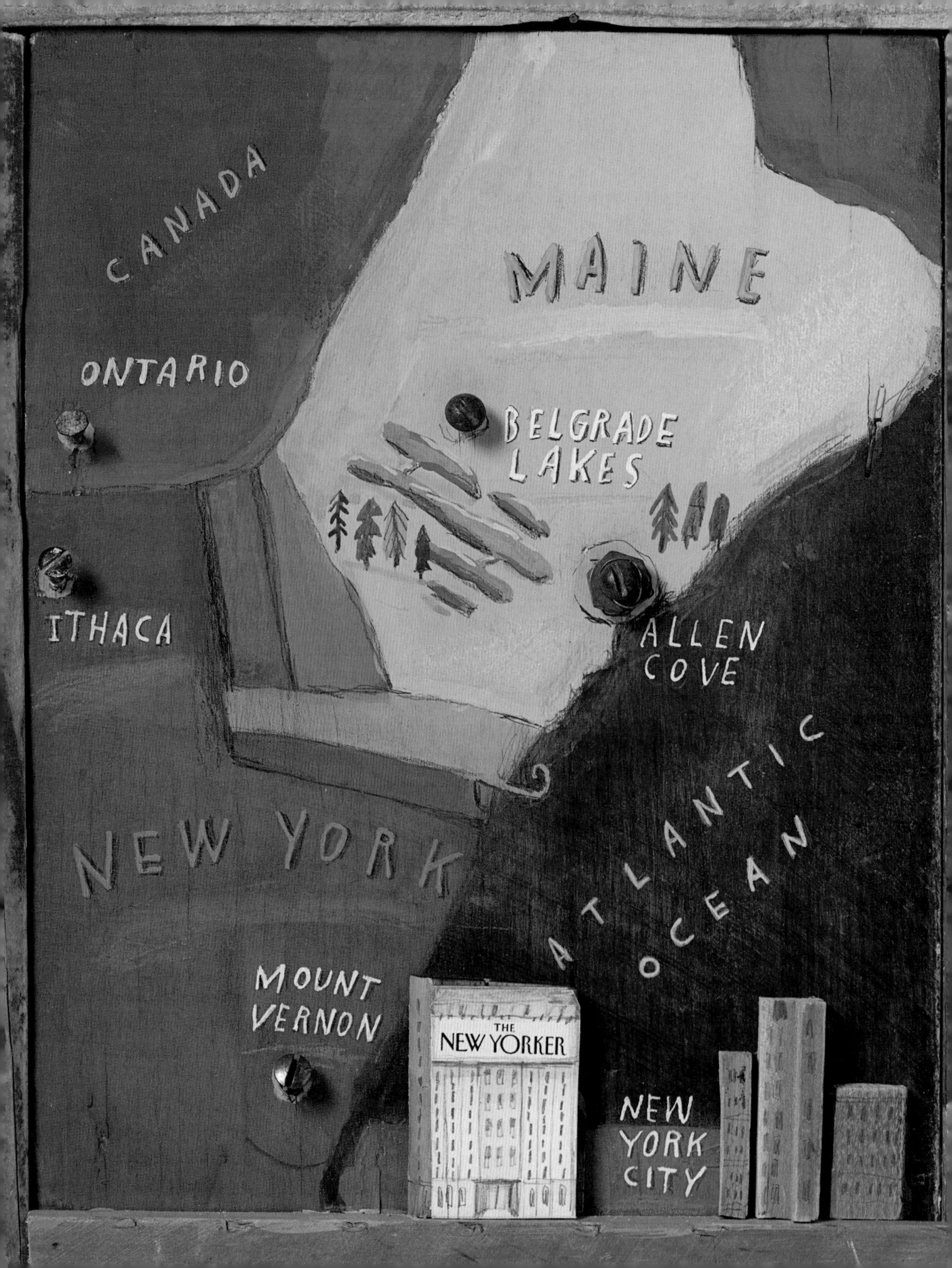
CANADA
MAINE
ONTARIO
BELGRADE LAKES
ITHACA
ALLEN COVE
ATLANTIC OCEAN
NEW YORK
MOUNT VERNON
THE NEW YORKER
NEW YORK CITY

Some Writer!

THE STORY OF E. B. WHITE

BY MELISSA SWEET

HOUGHTON MIFFLIN HARCOURT
BOSTON   NEW YORK

E.B.White
used a manual
typewriter....

CORONA

How a Manual Typewriter Works:

Insert a sheet of paper (1) onto a roller (2). Press a type key, such as (E) (3), and a lever (4) swings a type hammer (5), which strikes an inked ribbon (6), making a printed impression of the letter "E" onto the paper.

CONTENTS

There once was a boy from New York . . .
Elwyn on the steps of his Mount Vernon home, 1905.

ALL'S RIGHT WITH THE WORLD DEPARTMENT

I fell in love with the sound of an early typewriter
and have been stuck with it ever since.

ELWYN BROOKS WHITE became a writer while he was still wearing knickers. He was seven or eight years old when he looked a sheet of paper "square in the eyes" and thought, *"This is where I belong, this is it."*

He was born on July 11, 1899, and later chose seven and eleven as his lucky numbers. That same year in downtown New York City, not far from his home, a reservoir was being filled to make way for a new library with a children's room where En (as he was called) would later take out books.

En was about five years old when his brother Stan (whom the family called "Bun" because he could wiggle his nose like a bunny) taught him to read by sounding out words from the *New York Times*. If En came across a word he didn't know, his father made him look it up in *Webster's Dictionary*. At dinner his father, who loved words, recited limericks. All six children would try to finish the last line.

En, Albert, and Stan.

En's mother, Jessie, was quiet and kind. She loved her garden and raising broods of baby chicks. Each year at Christmas, she placed her "dream farm"—a tiny wooden farm—under the Christmas tree.

When he entered first grade, En discovered school began with an assembly. Every day after the students recited the Pledge of Allegiance and sang a song, the principal called a different student

En (note the fountain pen in his lapel pocket) and his mother.

to the platform to read aloud. He went in alphabetical order, and for years En sat in terror as the names got closer to *W*.

The day he heard "Elwyn White," En made his way to the stage and began reading a poem from Longfellow.

It had the line *Footprints on the sands of time*, but Elwyn's words came out *the tands of sime*. Other kids started laughing and the moment on stage became even worse than En had imagined it would be. He could not finish. He vowed never to go up on a stage again.

On his way home, his dog Mac met him as usual at the corner. In the quiet of the barn, En tended his chicks, his lizards, and his pigeons.

FOR SIX YEARS [Mac] met me at the same place after school and convoyed me home – a service he thought up himself. A boy doesn't forget that sort of association.

FROM ONE MAN'S MEAT
TITLE "Dog Training"
DATE 1940

En's dog, Mac.

A

S A CHILD, I was frightened but not unhappy. My parents were loving and kind. We were a large family...and were a small kingdom unto ourselves. Nobody ever came to dinner....We lived in a large house in a leafy suburb, where there were backyards and stables and grape arbors. I lacked for nothing except confidence. I suffered nothing except the routine terrors of childhood: fear of the dark, fear of the future, fear of the return to school after a summer on a lake in Maine, fear of making an appearance on a platform... fear that I was unknowing about things I should know about. I was, as a child, allergic to pollens and dusts, and still am....It may be, as some critics suggest, that it helps to have an unhappy childhood. If so, I have no knowledge of it.

FROM PARIS REVIEW

DATE 1969

The New York Times

Elwyn's father, Samuel White, worked at a piano company on Fifth Avenue in Manhattan. "One of the fringe benefits of being the son of a piano man," Elwyn wrote later, "was that our parlor at 101 Summit Avenue was well supplied with musical instruments." All six kids played instruments: "We were practically a ready-made band. All we lacked was talent. We had violins, cellos, mandolins, guitars, banjos, and drums, and there was always a lot of music filling the air in our home, none of it good. We sang, composed, harmonized, drummed . . . in an attempt to raise the general tone of the commotion."

Elwyn playing mandolin.

En was much younger than his siblings, so his father had more time to spend with him. "Oh, the joy, the joy of my little boy; we have lots of good times together!" Samuel White wrote to Albert. And for En's twelfth birthday, he gave him an optimistic note:

Elwyn, my dear boy,

All hail! with joy and gladness we salute you on your natal day. May each recurring anniversary bring you earth's best gifts and heaven's choicest blessings. Think today on your mercies. You have been born in the greatest and best land on the face of the globe under the best government known to men. Be thankful then that you are an American. Moreover you are the youngest child of a large family and have profited by the companionship of older brothers and sisters—this is no small matter for you are wiser by reason of their experiences. You haven't had to learn wisdom you have absorbed it. You are the object of the affectionate solicitude of your mother and father. . . . When you are fretted by the small things of life remember that on this your birthday you heard a voice telling you to look up and out on the great things of life and beholding them say—surely they are all mine. In conclusion, I congratulate you again and with my warmest felicitation I wish you great joy, I wish you all happiness and I wish it for you with all my heart.

Father

One Sunday afternoon, when En was about five years old, he and his family piled into a carriage for a ride. En started to sneeze; his eyes became red and itchy. His parents wondered if it was the horses, but they discovered En had hay fever and was allergic to pollen. The doctor prescribed dousing his head in cold water every morning.

Later that year, Samuel White went to visit Elwyn's older brothers, Al and Stan, who were staying with friends at a camp on the Belgrade Lakes in Maine. Would the crisp, clear air and cool lakes up north help En's hay fever? his father wondered. Mr. White made plans to take the whole family and their dog to Snug Harbor in Belgrade Lakes.

ONCE MORE TO THE LAKE

Life is always a rich and steady time when you are waiting for something to happen or to hatch.

GETTING TO MAINE was as much of an adventure as summering there. The family packed for one month and took a train overnight from New York City. Mrs. White slept fully dressed so she would be ready when they arrived in Belgrade Lakes early the next morning. From there, they took a horse and wagon ten miles to Snug Harbor. Mr. White had rented two small cabins at the edge of the lake.

"We Whites were city people," En later wrote. "Everything about Belgrade was a new experience: the big freshwater lake, the pines and spruces and birches, the pastures with its sweet-fern and juniper, the farmhouse where we took our meals, the rough camp with its sparsely furnished bedrooms . . . the boating, the swimming, and the company of other campers along the shore."

The White family motoring in Jessie *with En in the middle.*

During his "summer without end," as Elwyn later described it, Stan taught En how to paddle a canoe and use a jackknife. The brothers studied tortoises, turtles, tadpoles, and toads. In later years, they brought their homemade skiff, *Jessie* (named after Mrs. White, who couldn't swim and hated the water). No matter what the weather, the whole family crowded into the skiff and motored to town "like barn swallows in their nest." At Bean's store Mr. White bought a case of Moxie soda, assuring his family that the new drink Coca-Cola would never be as popular as Moxie.

En began keeping a journal (he thought the word "journal" sounded more writerly than "diary"). He wrote in his journal every day for the next twenty years.

IT WAS just a cheap notebook that was always by his bed. Every night, before he turned in, he would write in the book. He wrote about things he had done, things he had seen, and thoughts he had had. Sometimes he drew a picture. He always ended by asking himself a question so he would have something to think about while falling asleep.

FROM	THE TRUMPET OF THE SWAN
DATE	1970

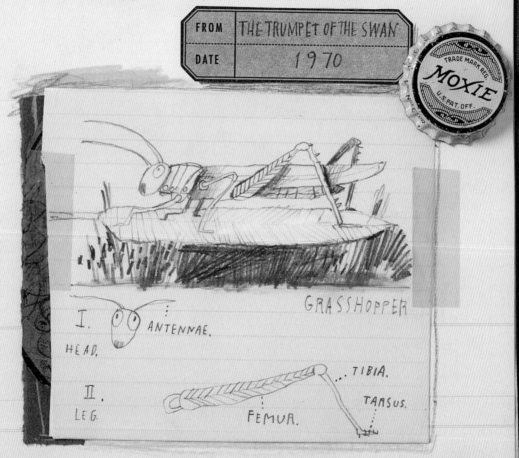

GRASSHOPPER

I. ANTENNAE.
HEAD.

II. ....TIBIA.
LEG. FEMUR. TARSUS.

I wonder what I'm going to be when I grow up?

Albert and En canoeing.

En and his father, about 1914.

For En's eleventh birthday, his father gave him a green wood-and-canvas Old Town canoe. Now the best part of the summer was not just being out of school but waking early, before the rest of the family, and sneaking out onto the lake in his own canoe. He would set out along the edge of the glassy lake in the shadows of the pines, paddling quietly so as not to disturb "the stillness of the cathedral," as he called the motionless water.

THERE WAS A lake, and at the water's edge a granite rock upholstered in lichen. This was his pew, and the sermon went on forever.

FROM	READERS DIGEST
TITLE	"A BOY I KNEW"
DATE	1940

One summer the Whites invited Elwyn's friend Freddie Schuler to join them in Maine. Fifteen-year-old Elwyn made Freddie a brochure to prepare him for "one of the most beautiful states in the Union, and . . . one of the most beautiful of the lakes of Maine." En wanted his friend to love Snug Harbor as much as he did.

Belgrade Lake

Maine is one of the most beautiful states in the Union, and Belgrade is one of the most beautiful of the lakes of Maine.

This wonderful lake is five miles wide, and about ten miles long, with many coves, points and islands. It is one

Samuel White, on the right in white shirt and tie.

Opposite: *En's front cover. Copy, layout, design, and publication by Elwyn B. White.*

Right: *Dedication inside the front to his friend Frederick "Freddie" Schuler, who lived across the street in Mount Vernon.*

This pamphlet was compiled by Elwyn B. White — It is respectfully dedicated to Mr. Frederick Schuler for his personal use.

Stanley canoeing.

of a series of lakes, whi
are connected with each
by little streams. One of
streams is several mile
and deep enough so that
affords an opportunity fo
fine all-day canoe trip

Elwyn learned cursive at about age seven.

of a series of lakes, which
are connected with each other
by little streams. One of these
streams is several miles long
and deep enough so that it
affords an opportunity for a
fine all-day canoe trip.
All the lakes are favorite
③

*Elwyn at the helm of Jessie.
The sixteen-foot skiff was built
by Albert and Stan.*

ideal for all kinds of small
boats. The bathing also is
a feature, for the days grow
very warm at noontime and
make a good swim feel fine.
⑤

resorts of fishermen, for bass, perch, chub, and pickerel are very plentiful.

The beauty of the surrounding country makes tramping a pleasure, and the well packed country roads are fine for bicycling and horse back riding.

The lake is large enough to make the conditions

④

While staying in Snug Harbor, the Whites ate their meals at a farmhouse down the road from their cottage.

The brochure was made with folded paper and bound with twine.

BELGRADE LAKE
AND
SNUG HARBOR CAMPS

Snug Harbor Camps

These camps are run by Mrs. Millard Gleason, North Belgrade, Maine. The price for a room and meals is twelve dollars a week. All necessities are furnished, including blankets.

The transportation, including baggage, berth, train ticket, breakfast, ride in to the lake, costs about twenty-five dollars, round trip.

At Snug Harbor Camps a doctor can always be quickly summoned from the boy's camp, which is only a mile away.

⑤

*Note the back cover logo for **B**elgrade **L**akes **M**aine.*

En later wrote of his summers in Maine, "The month of August was four solid weeks of heaven."

Freddie did join the Whites that summer, and he and
Elwyn spent their days fishing, canoeing, and swimming.
Much too soon, Elwyn knew, it would be time to go back
to school, but he also knew that when he returned the next
summer, the lake would be exactly as he had left it.

YEARS OF WONDER

I took to writing early, to assuage my uneasiness
and collect my thoughts, and I was a busy writer
long before I went into long pants.

ONE BY ONE, En's brothers and sisters left their home
in New York. Al and Stan graduated from Cornell
University, Lillian attended Vassar College, and his other
sisters married and had children—at five years old, En was
already an uncle!

Elwyn could canoe, ice-skate, play *Aida* on the piano,
and ride his bike backwards while sitting on the handlebars.
But girls terrified him.

He also liked to write poems, stories, and letters to his siblings, sometimes signing his letter "Sir Elwyn White" or "Buttercup." When he was nine, En sent a poem to Albert, his brother at Cornell, and a few months later En submitted it to a *Woman's Home Companion* contest—and won his first literary prize!

A STORY OF A LITTLE MOUSE
by Elwyn White

Once there was a wise little mouse,
At least that's what he thought,
But this experience shows you
Just what his wisdom brought.

One day as he walked through the kitchen,
A wire box he spied,
And in it was a hunk of cheese
Which he very carefully eyed.

Then he decided he'd have some
So in the box he stepped,
Farther and farther and farther
Very cautiously he crept.

But all of a sudden the trap sprang
And cut right off his head,
For the cruel trap had been laid for him
And there he lay quite dead.

As a lesson for a little mouse
I certainly advise,
That mice had better be careful,
And try not to be too wise.

In this letter written in 1908, En told Albert, "I wrote a poem about a little mouse . . . I am sorry I wrote that poem because I am trying to catch a mouse and that won't encourage them, will it?"

En began sending his stories to *St. Nicholas*, a monthly magazine for young readers. One of the magazine's most popular features was the St. Nicholas League contests held for the best stories, essays, poems, drawings, and snapshots and puzzles. If a piece was published, the artist would win a gold or silver badge. Anyone could join the League. Other budding writers—Edna St. Vincent Millay, William Faulkner, Eudora Welty, and Rachel Carson—were members. En later described the League members as "an industrious and fiendishly competitive band of tots."

A neighborhood friend, E. Barrett Brady, pointed out that the stories that won prizes were often about being kind to animals. All his life En had been kind to animals; he had tended to "pigeons,

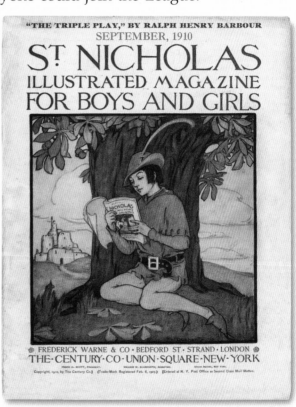

St. Nicholas *magazine, 1910.*

dogs, snakes, polliwogs, turtles, rabbits, lizards, singing birds, chameleons, caterpillars, and mice." So it wasn't hard for him to write a story about animals. When he wrote "A Winter Walk," about a dog and woodland animals, it won a silver badge from *St. Nicholas*. A few years later, "A True Dog Story," about his dog Beppo, won the coveted gold medal.

St. NICHOLAS LEAGUE

LIVE TO LEARN, AND LEARN TO LIVE

A TRUE DOG STORY

BY ELWYN B. WHITE (AGE 14)

(Gold Badge, Silver Badge won June 1911)

HE is a large Irish setter, with a beautiful red coat, and a lovable disposition. One summer when we were in Maine, Father and my two brothers went for a walk, taking Beppo, the dog with them. Coming to what seemed to be a large pasture slope, they climbed over the stone wall and walked up the hill. Just as they reached the summit, so they could see beyond, they were confronted by a large herd of steers. On seeing them, the animals advanced, menacingly. The trio started back to the wall with Beppo in leash, but found to their horror that the steers were chasing them. It would be impossible to reach the wall by running. There seemed to be but one way—the dog. On the farm, Beppo had been

A few years before En wrote "A True Dog Story," he had a word puzzle published in St. Nicholas. To find the answer to his "Cross-Word Enigma" (above right), turn to page 159.

CROSS-WORD ENIGMA

My *first* is in cup, but not in pail;
My *second* in story, but not in tale;
My *third* is in fresh, but not in stale;
My *fourth* is in conquer, but not in fail;
My *fifth* is in cell, but not in jail;
My *sixth* is in healthy and also in hale;
My *seventh*'s in sail and dale and mail;
My *whole* is a college; it is not Yale.

ELWYN B. WHITE (League Member).

ILLUSTRATED PRIMAL ACROSTIC

taught to bring in cows by going around in back of them, and chasing them on. The folks realized that if he did that now it would be fatal; and yet they must act and act quickly, for the big animals were rapidly coming upon them. Again they looked at the wall—it seemed a quarter of a mile away. There was but one thing to do. Setting the dog loose, my brother cried, "Hold 'em Bep; hold 'em!" Simultaneously the dog bounded toward the herd, and the three made for the wall. For about two hundred yards they ran as they had never run before. Then looking over their shoulders, they saw the whole herd standing on the brow of the hill, with a little ball of red racing madly up and down in front of them. In a minute, the little party was safely over the wall, and Beppo, the hero, came barking down the hill.

In high school, En began writing for the *Oracle*, his school newspaper. But the best part of high school, he said, "was getting to and fro, which was on my bicycle." Girls may have noticed him, but he didn't have the nerve to ask them out.

En was still in high school when World War I broke out. He had his heart set on going to Cornell University, just like his brothers, and was accepted and awarded scholarships that more than

DO I LOOK LIKE THAT ?

En, as a young teenager, with his own caption beneath the photograph.

covered the hundred-dollar-a-year tuition. Still, in 1917, the summer before Elwyn went to college, he wrote in his journal:

> *May 27. I don't know what to do this summer. The country is at war and I think I ought to serve.*
> *July 5. My utter dependence galls me, and I am living the life of a slacker.*

But En didn't weigh enough to join the army. Finally, he joined the cadets and worked on a farm for the summer. Even though he was about to leave for Cornell in the fall, his journal entry on his birthday was no more enthusiastic:

> *July 11. Eighteen and still no future! I'd be more contented in prison, for there at least I would know precisely what I had to look forward to.*

DIDN'T CARE for athletics, being skinny
and small, but I liked ice ponds and skating,
and on winter afternoons and evenings I would
visit a pond (a fifteen-minute ride on a
trolley car) and skate with a girl named
Mildred Hesse....Together we must have covered
hundreds of miles, sometimes leaving the pond
proper and gliding into the woods on narrow
fingers of ice. We didn't talk much, never
embraced, we just skated for the ecstasy of
skating - a magical glide....This brief inter-
lude on ice...had a dreamlike quality, a
purity, that has stayed with me all my life;
and when nowadays I see a winter sky and feel
the wind dropping with the sun and the
naked trees against a reddening west, I
remember what it was like to be in love
before any of love's complexities or realities
or disturbances had entered in, to dilute
its splendor and challenge its perfection.

FROM   LETTERS OF E.B. WHITE
DATE   1976

Elwyn arrived at Cornell University in Ithaca, New York, a few days before classes started. He checked in to a hotel to wait, and in his enthusiasm, he became so engrossed in what was going on in town—the trolleys, the walking paths, and Lake Cayuga—that days went by before he realized classes had already begun.

Elwyn White, about 1917.

Elwyn liked Cornell. His classmates nicknamed him "Andy," after Cornell's first president, Andrew Dickson White. From then on, to friends and family, Elwyn White was Andy White.

His professors became part of his social life. Students met at Professor Adams's house for cocoa and chess. Andy joined Professor Sampson's Manuscript Club; from Professor Strunk he learned to "omit needless words" in his writing; and he fell in love with Henry David Thoreau's *Walden*. Andy began writing for the school newspaper, the *Cornell Sun*, which he found much more interesting than studying. (He got a D in English his second semester.) When he became editor of the *Sun*, it took so much of his time, he was excused from his English class. He wrote his mother, "This morning came news

I'D SEND MY son to Cornell... because Will Strunk, Jr. is there...I'd send him there to walk up Six Mile Creek in the early wetness of a recalcitrant Spring.

FROM E.B. WHITE: A BIOGRAPHY

DATE 1985

Professor William Strunk, Jr. taught English from a book he wrote: The Elements of Style.

DARWIN WAS RIGHT

ME STUDYING

Andy White at Cornell, with his own captions beneath the photos. He loved the streams and lakes around Ithaca. About Will Strunk he wrote that his professor was "a memorable man, friendly and funny."

of my utter redemption from my deepest gloom . . . which is merely to say I don't have to write so much stuff every day."

One year Andy took a class in medieval history. The professor, George Lincoln Burr, taught in such a way that Andy was "transported" back centuries. He learned that when tyrants reign, societies sacrifice freedom. In Andy's senior year, it was Burr who stood up for a Cornell student who was being bullied into wearing a "freshman cap" (a tradition upperclassmen had come up with for all freshmen). The student had refused to wear it, and the campus was in an uproar. But Burr observed: "A matter of garb seems to me a small thing to fight about. . . . What chance for discussion? What room for protest? . . . There is no safety valve so precious to civil order as legitimate freedom of thot [*sic*] and speech."

Andy said that meeting Burr "was the single greatest thing that ever happened" in his life. Burr introduced Andy to a part of himself he had not yet discovered; Andy saw, "with blinding clarity,"

Professor George Lincoln Burr.

how important it was to live with the freedom to express ideas. "To be free," Andy wrote later, "is to feel you belong to the earth." For the first time, Andy had a focus for his thoughts, for his principles. He began to consider writing for a living.

After graduation, Andy took a job as a counselor at Camp Otter, in Canada. A classmate from Cornell, Howard "Cush" Cushman, went too. Neither wanted to rush into a job in an office. Maybe they would go out west for a while. What was the hurry to have a regular job?

Andy White (with his first mustache), pictured third from right, at Camp Otter in Ontario, 1921.

FROM SEA TO SHINING SEA

A person who is looking for something doesn't travel very fast.

WHEN HE RETURNED home from camp, Andy had a series of writing jobs that he disliked. He and Cush made plans to go west. Andy bought a Model T roadster for about four hundred dollars and named it Hotspur. He and Cush organized camping gear and packed their clothes, a cigar-box fiddle, two Corona typewriters, and a *Webster's Dictionary*—to remind them their "true destination was the world of letters." Andy said nothing about this trip to his parents.

The night before they were ready to leave, Cush joined Andy at the Whites' house for dinner. At the supper table, Andy announced they were heading out west in the morning, leaving no time for his parents to talk him out of the trip. Andy and Cush had no real plan except to go west and pay their way by writing as they went along.

They were in no hurry. In 1922, the roads that crossed America were sometimes just paths through fields. Signs were often arrows made from old shingles. They deliberately didn't even pack a road map. Like Thoreau, still a favorite author of Andy's, they were "travelling light and trying new adventures."

THE MODEL T was not a fussy car. It sprang cheerfully toward any stretch of wasteland whether there was a noticeable road under foot or not....The course of my life was changed by it, and it is in a class by itself. It was cheap enough so I could afford to buy one; it was capable enough so it gave me courage to start.

FROM FROM SEA TO SHINING SEA

DATE 1953

Cush in Hotspur, in Montana, 1922.

Townsend
WASHINGTON
SEATTLE
TACOMA
OLYMPIA
Columbia
ARRIVE
Seattle
October
1922
6
Cush and Andy.
4
$7
5
CANADA
3
2
MINNEAPOLIS JOURNAL
LIMERICK CONTEST
A young man who liked to rock boats
In order to get people's goats
Gave just one more rock
Then suffered a shock
A bubble the spot now denotes.
UNITED
MEXICO

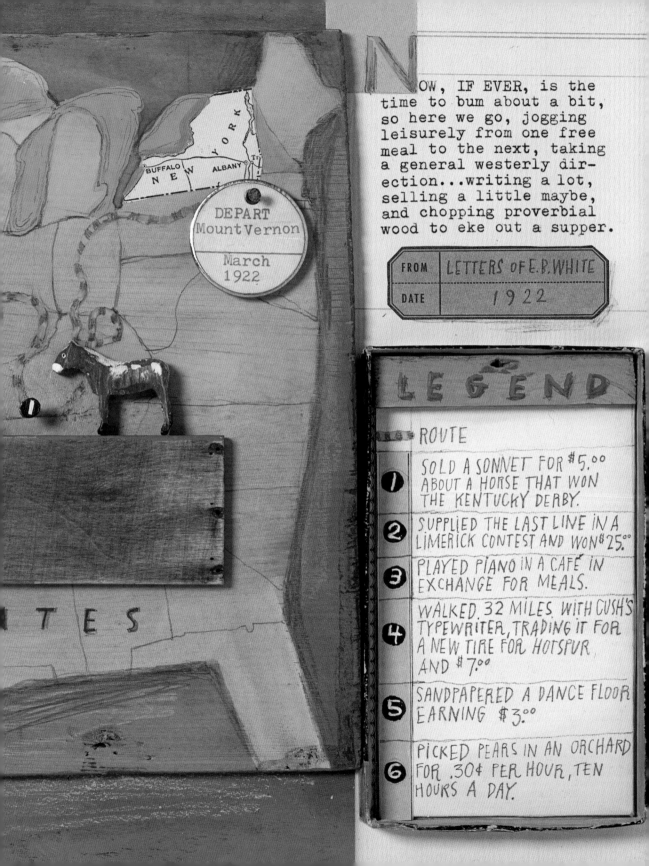

OW, IF EVER, is the time to bum about a bit, so here we go, jogging leisurely from one free meal to the next, taking a general westerly direction...writing a lot, selling a little maybe, and chopping proverbial wood to eke out a supper.

FROM	LETTERS of E.B. WHITE
DATE	1922

DEPART
Mount Vernon

March
1922

BUFFALO
NEW YORK   ALBANY

LEGEND

ROUTE

① SOLD A SONNET FOR $5.00 ABOUT A HORSE THAT WON THE KENTUCKY DERBY.

② SUPPLIED THE LAST LINE IN A LIMERICK CONTEST AND WON $25.00

③ PLAYED PIANO IN A CAFÉ IN EXCHANGE FOR MEALS.

④ WALKED 32 MILES WITH CUSH'S TYPEWRITER, TRADING IT FOR A NEW TIRE FOR HOTSPUR, AND $7.00

⑤ SANDPAPERED A DANCE FLOOR EARNING $3.00

⑥ PICKED PEARS IN AN ORCHARD FOR .30¢ PER HOUR, TEN HOURS A DAY.

THAT AFTERNOON WE washed dirt from ourselves and our clothes in Ten Mile Lake and slept there in a little pine grove.

FROM | LETTERS OF E.B. WHITE
DATE | 1922

Tuesday, June 27, 1922

Andy White, reporter,
Seattle Times, 1923.

As a reporter (and later columnist),
he earned forty dollars per week, but
discovered he would "never make a
good newspaper reporter . . . I was
not quick enough or alert enough.
I was always taking the wrong train
in the wrong direction."

When they arrived in Seattle six months later, Andy wrote that he had left "a track across the United States as erratic as a mouse's track in snow." He found a job as a reporter with the *Seattle Times*. Cush headed back home. As a reporter, Andy hated to be told what to write, but he liked his boss. When Andy asked how to describe a story, his boss thought for a moment and then said: "Just say the words." It was sound advice that Andy remembered the rest of his life.

The *Seattle Times* gave him a chance to write small personal pieces, but eventually Andy was laid off. That was fine with him. He preferred to be footloose. Andy took a ship to Alaska and Siberia before heading home.

On returning to New York, he lived with his parents and commuted to a new job in advertising in Manhattan. Andy still sent out his light verses, sonnets, and squibs to magazines, mostly for no pay—just for the "sheer glory" of sometimes seeing his writing in print. At night, on Long Island Sound, he sailed his canoe rigged with "sails made of bed sheets."

Then a friend told him about a brand-new magazine that might like Andy's sense of humor. In February of 1925, Andy "swung into Grand Central Terminal . . . laid fifteen cents on the line," and bought the very first issue of *The New Yorker*. Nine weeks later, the new magazine published a piece by E. B. White.

The first New Yorker *cover, with art by Rea Irvin, 1925.*

5

ANSWERS TO HARD QUESTIONS

```
I discovered...that writing of the small things of
the day, the trivial matters of the heart...was the
only kind of creative work which I could accomplish
with any sincerity or grace.
```

???

ANDY CALLED HIMSELF a "short writer." He described the *New Yorker* pieces as "short, relaxed, and sometimes funny." The magazine set out to create a witty weekly about life in New York City. With each issue they produced, the *New Yorker* editors were figuring out what kind of magazine it would be. No one predicted that this magazine filled with sassy cartoons would become one of the preeminent literary journals in America.

That year, *The New Yorker* published more of Andy's writing, but he still sent his work to other newspapers and magazines, including *New York World*, which had a column called *The Conning Tower*. For a young writer to see his work in the *Tower*, as Andy called it, was a high point, a "moment in the sun."

In the summer of 1926, Andy moved into an apartment in Greenwich Village with three Cornell classmates. Though he wanted people to read his work, he didn't feel obligated to mingle with other writers. He liked how the city gave him "the gift of loneliness and the gift of privacy."

Both Harold Ross, publisher of *The New Yorker,* and the fiction editor Katharine Sergeant Angell noticed Andy's writings in other journals. They asked Andy to work part time at *The New Yorker* as a staff writer. Though Andy met with them and continued to send *The New Yorker* his writing, he had a better offer.

Harold Ross

The Conning Tower

FOR THINGS THAT ARE A PART OF ME

When days, by ending, make me old;
When neither fortune comes nor gold;
When love, with eyes that speak the truth,
Backs slowly from me, like my youth,
And friends who know their way alone
Go forth and leave me, one by one;
Still must I very thankful be
For things that are a part of me:
That when I read a pretty line
A little flame goes down my spine,
That when I see the morning sun
I laugh to think the world's begun.

E. B. W.

Andy's poem in the New York World.

One of his roommates had a job making a promotional movie for the Cunard cruise line and was headed to Europe. At nine o'clock one morning, he told Andy that in exchange for writing a movie script, he would earn forty-five dollars a week and would get to go on the cruise. At five o'clock that same day, they sailed to Europe. Just before Andy left, he sent out a poem to *The Conning Tower*. Katharine Sergeant Angell saw the published poem and wrote again to Andy, but he had already set sail.

THE NEW YORKER

25 WEST 45TH STREET

NEW YORK CITY

July 15, 1926.

Mr. Elwyn Brooks White,
112 West 13th Street,
New York, New York.

Dear Mr. White:

The New Yorker looks with jealous eyes
at your verse that led off The Conning Tower
this week, and we all like it so much that we say,
alas, that you did not send it to us. Mr. Ross
and I are wondering whether you won't call up some
day to have lunch with us perhaps or at least ar-
range to drop in at the office to discuss various
thoughts we have in mind for you in connection with
The New Yorker. Won't you do us the favor of giving
us a ring?

Sincerely yours,

THE NEW YORKER

K. S. Angell.

KSA.DC

Letter to E. B. White from Katharine Sergeant Angell, 1926.

When the ship returned to New York six weeks later, Andy debarked, picked up his mail, then walked to Childs' Restaurant. While waiting for his dinner, he opened envelopes containing checks from *The New Yorker*—nearly $178 spilled out, payment for pieces he had sent in before he left. At last, he was being paid to write exactly as he pleased. Eventually, Harold Ross convinced Andy to work

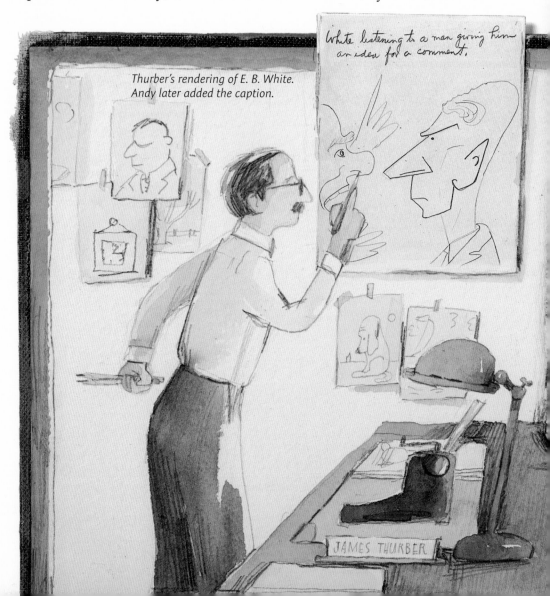

Thurber's rendering of E. B. White. Andy later added the caption.

at *The New Yorker*. He earned just thirty dollars a week, and for a time he had to get another job to make ends meet. Andy shared an office barely big enough for "two desks, two typewriters, and a mountainous stack of yellow copy paper" with another writer he barely knew: James Thurber. Andy was as reserved as Thurber was gregarious. "From the first, we loved each other's stuff," Andy said.

Andy's writing was becoming more popular. Thurber wrote that when someone came to the *New Yorker* offices wanting to meet E. B. White, Andy would "slip moodily out of the building by way of the fire escape and hide in Schrafft's [restaurant] until the visitor went away."

Thurber wrote the way a child skips rope, the way a mouse waltzes.

NO ONE CAN WRITE A SENTENCE LIKE WHITE... HE MADE ME REALIZE A WRITER TURNS ON HIS MIND, NOT A FAUCET.

E. B. White and James Thurber, 1929. Within a year of their meeting, Andy wrote in his journal, "One of the persons I like best in the world is Thurber."

White's job was writing captions for cartoons, short articles on current events called "Comments," and "Newsbreaks"—humorous column fillers that poked fun at errors and typos in other magazines and newspapers.

"There is a secret joy in discovering a blunder in the public prints," Andy wrote. "Almost every person has a little of the proofreader in him."

Andy scanned newspapers and magazines for mistakes, typos, and "blunders." Readers also sent in clippings from all over the country. He then sometimes gave the Newsbreak a headline from the list of "Newsbreak Department Heads," written by Andy and the staff. The punch line following a Newsbreak was called a "snapper."

NEATEST TRICK OF THE WEEK
[From the Kansas City Star]

PHILADELPHIA, OCT. 1.—A 36-year-old New York school teacher became the bride of a 77-year-old New York minister and the father of nine children here today.

Left: *Note the headline from the Newsbreak list opposite.*

Below: *Note the "snappers" following the two Newsbreaks.*

In last week's issue some errors were made regarding Mrs. Gillcuddy, which the following account will correct: Mrs. Gilcuddy was born in 1865, and was 64 years and 11 days of age at the time of her birth.—*Santa Ana (Cal.) Record.*

There! Now *that's* straight.

Q. I have only been married four months and sure got an ideal husband. We have an acre of land and are real happy, except that my husband makes me so nervous by walking in his sleep and he tries to get out of the window. Last night he carried all the clothes on the front porch. I can't understand this. It seems to be a dream. Is there any way to overcome this awful thing? When he does this I can hardly breathe. Please tell me what to do.—YOUNG WIFE.—*Los Angeles Express.*

The first thing to do is get over the notion that you have an ideal husband.

NEWSBREAK DEPARTMENT HEADS

ALL'S RIGHT WITH THE WORLD DEPARTMENT

ANSWERS TO HARD QUESTIONS

ANTICLIMAX DEPARTMENT

A THOUGHT FOR THIS WEEK

Balderdash Department

BLOCK THAT METAPHOR!

BRAVE NEW WORLD DEPARTMENT

BROTHERHOOD OF MAN DEPT.

CLEAR DAYS ON THE POLITICAL SCENE

Contributory Notes from All Over

DEPARTMENT OF BELLES-LETTRES

DEPARTMENT OF DELICACY

DEPARTMENT OF ELEGANCE

DEPT. OF ENGLISH LITERATURE

DEPT. OF HIGHER EDUCATION

DEPT. OF STRAIGHT THINKING

DEPT. OF UNDERSTATEMENT

DEPT. OF UTTER CONFUSION

DON'T GIVE IT A SECOND THOUGHT DEPARTMENT

FULLER EXPLANATION DEPT.

FUNNY COINCIDENCE DEPARTMENT

GO CLIMB A TREE DEPARTMENT

HIGHER MATHEMATICS DEPT.

HO-HUM DEPARTMENT

HOOPLA DEPARTMENT

HOW'S THAT AGAIN? DEPARTMENT

INFATUATION WITH SOUND OF OWN WORDS DEPARTMENT

IT'S ABOUT TIME DEPARTMENT

[LAUGHTER] ON CAPITOL HILL

LETTERS WE NEVER FINISHED READING

LIFE IN HOLLYWOOD DEPARTMENT

LOVE IS A WONDERFUL THING DEPARTMENT

MOST FASCINATING NEWS STORY OF THE WEEK

MR. CARLYLE, MEET MR. EMERSON

NEATEST TRICK OF THE WEEK

NO COMMENT DEPARTMENT

NON-SEQUITUR DEPARTMENT

NON-STOP SENTENCE DERBY

No Vivid Writing. Please

NO SOONER SAID THAN DONE DEPT.

ONCE A LADY ALWAYS A LADY DEPARTMENT

ONE WORLD DEPARTMENT

O PIONEERS DEPARTMENT

OUR FORGETFUL AUTHORS

OUR HUNGRY CRITICS

OUR OWN BUSINESS DIRECTORY

PERISH THE THOUGHT DEPT.

POESY DEPARTMENT

PROSE PASSAGES WE HATED TO COME TO THE END OF

PSHAW DEPARTMENT

PYRRHIC VICTORY DEPARTMENT

RAISED EYEBROWS DEPARTMENT

REMARKABLE REMARKS

REMARKS WE DOUBT EVER GOT MADE

RICH, BEAUTIFUL PROSE DEPT.

Sentences We Hated to Come to the End Of

RIP VAN WINKLE DEPARTMENT

SILVER LINING DEPARTMENT

SLIGHT HEADACHE DEPARTMENT

SOCIAL NOTES FROM ALL OVER

STATISTICAL DEPARTMENT

TCH, TCH DEPARTMENT

THAT'S TOO BAD DEPARTMENT

THE BUREAUCRATIC MIND AT WORK

THE CLOUDED CRYSTAL BALL

THE CREATIVE LIFE

THE GOOD OLD DAYS

THE LEGAL MIND AT WORK

THE LITERARY LIFE

THE LYRICAL PRESS

THE MYSTERIOUS EAST

THE NEW ARMY

THE PUBLISHING LIFE

THERE'LL ALWAYS BE AN ADMAN

THERE'LL ALWAYS BE AN ENGLAND

THIS CHANGING WORLD

THIS IS WAR

UH-HUH DEPARTMENT

UP LIFE'S LADDER

WE DON'T WANT TO HEAR ABOUT IT DEPARTMENT

WHAT PAPER D'YA READ?

WIND ON CAPITOL HILL DEPT.

WORDS OF ONE SYLLABLE DEPT.

SENTENCES WE LOST INTEREST IN BEFORE GETTING VERY FAR

THE NEW YORKER—43612—NEWSBREAK DEPT. HEADS—MARCH 17, 1976

The New Yorker's list of "Newsbreak Departments Heads". Note E. B. White's handwritten additions.

Most of the staff worked a typical ten-to-five day, but Andy came and went as he pleased. He sometimes took off for Maine without telling anyone where he was going. But he always made his deadlines.

One spring Andy was traveling home from Virginia on a train and fell asleep. He dreamt of a mouse who was fully dressed in dapper clothing with a hat and cane. Andy wrote it all down. Later, when one of his eighteen nieces and nephews wanted a story, Andy would read it aloud. He named the mouse Stuart, and kept the story in a drawer, sometimes adding new episodes.

At *The New Yorker*, Andy and Thurber and Katharine Sergeant Angell became fast friends. And though it didn't happen right away, Andy and Katharine fell in love. Katharine, however, was married with two children. But her marriage had been unhappy long before she met Andy. Eventually, she got divorced. Her children from that marriage, Roger and Nancy, would live with their father during the school year and with Katharine in the summers.

Finally, one autumn, Andy and Katharine were married in a small ceremony—just the two of them and their dog Daisy, a present from Thurber. But Daisy got into a scuffle with the minister's dog. "It was a very nice wedding," Andy wrote. "Nobody threw anything and there was a dog fight." They were both back at work the next day.

Katharine Sergeant Angell, born and raised in Boston, graduated from Bryn Mawr College. Harold Ross described her as "irreplaceable."

Andy later wrote of his first meeting with Katharine: "I sat there peacefully gazing at the classic features of my future wife without, as usual, knowing what I was doing."

Andy wrote the poem below for Katharine from Ontario, 1929.

Natural History

The spider, dropping down from twig,
Unwinds a thread of his devising:
A thin, premeditated rig
To use in rising.

And all the journey down through space,
In cool descent, and loyal-hearted,
He builds a ladder to the place
From which he started.

Thus I, gone forth, as spiders do,
In spider's web a truth discerning,
Attach one silken strand to you
For my returning.

FROM: LETTERS OF E.B. WHITE

DATE: 1929

E.B. White slowly accustomed himself to the idea that he had made the most beautiful decision of his life.

In May, when they learned Katharine was pregnant, Andy was so overcome with joy, he didn't know how to express himself, so he had their dog, Daisy, "write" a letter to Katharine. Daisy wrote, "What [White] feels, he told me, is a strange queer tight little twitchy feeling around the inside of his throat whenever he thinks that something is happening which will require so much love and all on account of you being so wonderful."

In December, they had a son, Joel "Joe" McCoun White.

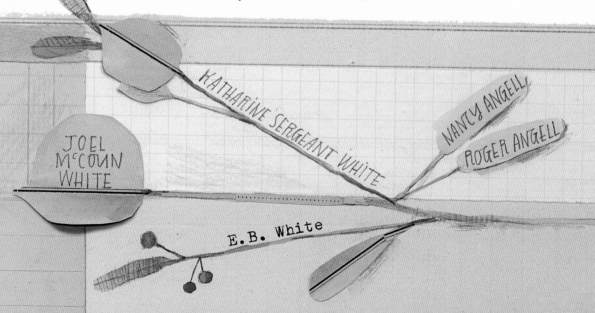

JOEL McCOUN WHITE

KATHARINE SERGEANT WHITE

NANCY ANGELL

ROGER ANGELL

E.B. White

SOME DAY WHEN I'm out of sight
Travel far but travel light!
Stalk the turtle on the log,
Watch the heron spear the frog,
Find the things you only find
When you leave your bag behind;
Raise the sail your old man furled,
Hang your hat upon the world!...

Joe, my tangible creation,
Happy in perambulation,
Work no harder than you have to.
        Do you get me?

FROM   THE CONNING TOWER

TITLE   "Apostrophe to a Pram Rider"

DATE   1931

Katharine White (with Joel in the pram) and the Whites' dog Daisy, 1931.

TO A WRITER,
a child is an alibi.
If I should never in
all my years write
anything worth reading,
I can always explain
that by pointing to
my child.

FROM	LETTERS OF E.B. WHITE
DATE	1931

Andy with Joel White, 1931.

Even though America was now in the Great Depression, a time when many people lost their homes and businesses and had trouble finding work, Katharine and Andy kept their jobs at *The New Yorker* and were paid well. Katharine was especially lucky, as few women had jobs in publishing at that time. One summer, Andy and Katharine took Roger, Nancy, and Joel on a vacation, loading up their Buick sedan with everything from a playpen to a nine-and-a-half-foot dinghy. It was the first of their many summers spent in Maine.

On one sailing trip along the coast of Maine, they anchored in a small cove in Blue Hill Bay. Directly in front was a rambling farm with a barn—just the kind of barn Andy had kept animals in while growing up on Summit Avenue. The next day, while driving down the road, they saw a For Sale sign in front of this very house and barn. The Whites immediately bought the farm and the surrounding forty acres for eleven thousand dollars. In time, a spider, a pig, a gaggle of geese, and all the other animals (including a rat) that E. B. White was about to acquire would make that barn famous.

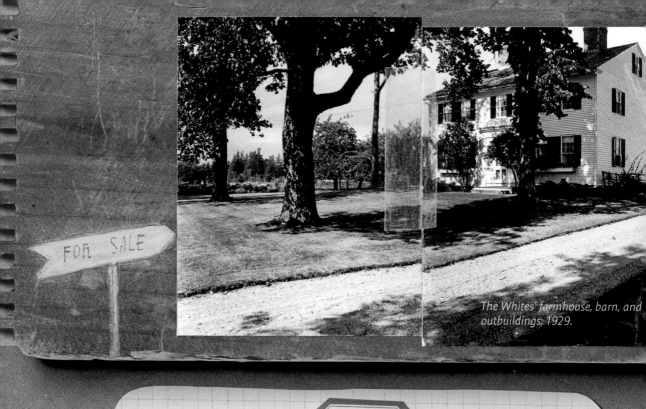

FOR SALE

The Whites' farmhouse, barn, and outbuildings, 1929.

MAP
OF WHITE
FARM

to →
BOAT
HOUSE

ALLEN COVE

HOUSE ↑   BARN

COWS→

BARNYARD

SHEEP ↑

PIG PEN

LANE TO PASTURE

ORCHARD ↓

to DUMP
↓

WHAT HAPPENS TO me when I cross...into
Maine...? I cannot describe it....but I do
have the sensation of having received a
gift from a true love.

FROM POINTS OF MY COMPASS
TITLE "Home-Coming"
DATE   1955

6

A TIME OF ENCHANTMENT

When I got a place in the country I was quite
sure animals would appear, and they did.

ANDY BECAME RESTLESS. He told Katharine he wanted
to be more than a successful *New Yorker* writer. In an
article about the Great Depression, Andy wrote, "The hope I
see for the world . . . is to simplify life." His parents had died
within a short time of each other. World War II was under
way. Andy had recently been criticized for writing about the

war but not offering any solutions. He was uneasy with the celebrity of writers in New York City and frustrated with *The New Yorker*'s policy that editorial writers had to write from the point of view of "we." He didn't like having his articles sound as if more than one person had written them. Andy wanted to write from his own point of view about whatever he wanted, and he wanted to do it in Maine. Disenchanted, he took a year off and went by himself to Maine to write—"My Year," as he called it—but he wrote only one long poem.

When he returned to New York, Andy convinced Katharine that they could both work from Maine. Joel would attend the local two-room schoolhouse. Within a few days of Andy's announcing he was leaving New York and *The New Yorker* (although he agreed to continue editing Newsbreaks), the editors of *Harper's Magazine* asked him if he would write essays from Maine for the magazine. They'd call his column *One Man's Meat*. He had to write only one piece every month, and, more important, he could write about anything and everything that interested him.

In Maine, Andy composed his essays for *Harper's* while tending the animals, shingling his barn, fishing with Joel. "The best writing," he said, "is often done by persons who are snatching time from something else."

Joel liked their new life in Maine too. There was time for skating, sledding, and sailing. Andy rigged a rope swing in the barn for Joel and built him his first boat: a flat-bottomed scow named *Flounder*. (The boat plans came from a book Andy had kept since childhood.) When his parents asked Joel what the biggest difference was between his "school-in-country" and his "school-in-city," he answered that in Maine, the days went by "just like lightning."

Above left: *Joel White teaching his dog Raffles to pull a berry basket.*
"E. B. White purchased a 25-cent ticket, and won Raffles, a wire-haired fox terrier puppy. He brought him home in his pocket and gave him to Joel."

Above right: *Joel at about age ten, driving the hay truck with Raffles.*

I HAVE discovered, rather too late in life, that there is nothing so much fun as building a boat. The best thing about building a boat is that it allows absolutely no time for writing; there isn't a minute to spare.

FROM LETTERS OF E.B. WHITE
DATE 1944

bottom, nail a ¾-inch long bottom board (Fig
Next cut two small boards of ¾-inch plank; mak
wide and about 1 foot 5 inches long; cut out a ace in one
end of each, as shown by A, Fig. 76; these are to re as row-

FIG. 75.

locks, and should be nailed with wrought-iron na
of the boat, so that the centres of the rowlocks are about 4
10 inches from the end which will be the stern of the boat; this
is the simplest style of rowlock, but a much neater one can be
made by using thole-pins (Fig. 77, B).

Turn the boat upon its side and nail a strip 11 feet long, 2
inches wide, and 1 inch thick upon the upper edge of the side
board; repeat the operation on the other side, using wrought
nails and clinching them. If thole-pins are intended to be used,

A

FIG. 76.

before nailing the strips upon the sides, 4 feet 9 inches from
one end of each strip cut a notch in the side ½ inch deep
and 1½ wide; 3 inches from this notch, or 5 feet from the same
end, cut another similar notch. When these strips are nailed on

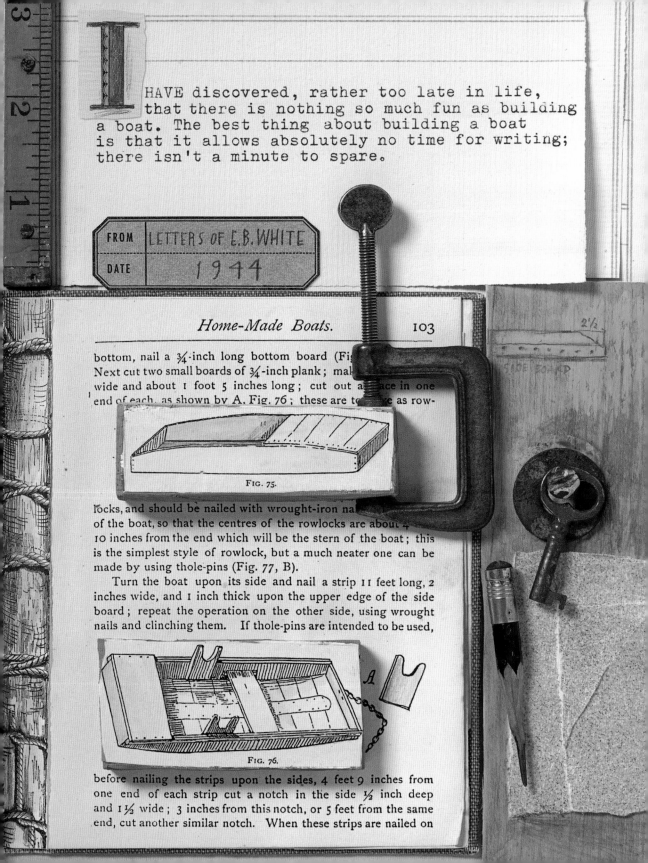

THE SCOW WAS Joe's first solo experience with
the water. I built her from a picture in the
<u>American Boy's Handy Book</u>, using pluck in place
of know-how, and when she glided into the frog
pond...and Joe dancing around, it was my finest
hour.

FROM LETTERS OF E.B. WHITE
DATE 1983

Part of Katharine's job at *The New Yorker* was reviewing children's books for a column she titled Children's Shelf. Review copies poured into the Whites' farmhouse. Books were piled everywhere: inside cupboards, under cushions, on stair landings. In an essay for *Harper's* called "Children's Books," Andy wrote that he'd found himself flat on his stomach reading about how to build a treehouse (the final touch was to include a small radio). Andy wrote, "It must be a lot of fun to write for children—reasonably easy work, perhaps even important work."

When Andy was growing up he read "with a passionate interest" all the books by William J. Long, a naturalist who wrote about animals in the wilds of Maine. But as an adult, he found most of the children's books "dull"—except for one: *The 500 Hats of Bartholomew Cubbins*, by Dr. Seuss. This book seemed to him to be in the "true spirit of nonsense."

Andy's essay about children's books caught the eye of Theodor Geisel (Dr. Seuss), who sent it to Anne Carroll Moore. Moore was a book reviewer and a children's librarian at the New York Public Library on Fifth Avenue—the library where the famous statues of two lions sit out front, and the library from which Andy had taken out books as a boy.

After Moore read the *Harper's* essay, she sent Katharine and Andy a letter urging Andy to write a children's book: "I feel sure you could, if you would, and I assure you the Library Lions would roar with all their praise." Andy didn't want to be prodded, but he happened to have that story about a mouse tucked away in a drawer. He later wrote James Thurber, who was now a preeminent cartoonist and writer, "I have a children's book half done."

Months later, Andy sent an unfinished manuscript to Eugene "Gene" Saxton, his editor at Harper and Brothers, which published Andy's adult books. He told Saxton that this story "would seem to be for children, but I'm not fussy who reads it." He added, "You will be shocked and grieved to discover that the principal character in the story has somewhat the attributes and appearance of a mouse." Saxton was not grieved—he could hardly wait. But it would be another six years before Stuart Little was born.

Stuart ~~Little~~ Little

but surprised to get such a small one.

the family were pleased to get a boy-baby

When the ~~this~~ ~~good~~ second Littles son was born he was not much bigger than a mouse – He looked a good deal like a mouse too with a sharp nose, pleasant eyes, & he carried and came to be regarded as one. a small cane. First you gained less than a third of an ounce, which worried his mother so she called the Doctor – who took Stuart's temperature & found that it was 98.6 which is normal for a mouse. ~~Feed him~~ He also examined Stuart's chest & heart. & looked into his ears solemnly with a tiny flashlight. It is ~~took~~ quite a thing to look into a mouse's ear without laughing Everything seemed to all right &

Stuart's mother was pleased to get such a good report.

"Feed him up!" said the

Early draft of Stuart Little, about 1935.

NCE IN everyone's life there is apt to
be a period when he is fully awake instead of
half asleep. I think of those five years in
Maine as the time when this happened to me.
Confronted by new challenges, surrounded by
new acquaintances - including the characters
in the barnyard who were later to appear
in Charlotte's Web - I was suddenly seeing,
feeling, and listening as a child sees,
feels and listens. It was one of those
rare interludes that can never be repeated,
a time of enchantment. I am fortunate indeed
to have had the chance to get some of it
down on paper.

FROM ONE MAN'S MEAT

DATE 1982

7

STUART LITTLE

My innocent tale of the quest for beauty.

URING WORLD WAR II, many people who were working at *The New Yorker* left the magazine to help with the war effort. Harold Ross was so understaffed that Andy and Katharine moved back to New York for a time to help him keep the magazine running. Joel went to a private school in New Hampshire. Katharine nagged Andy to finish *Stuart Little*. Anne Carroll Moore nagged too. When his editor nagged Andy about getting the book out, Andy wrote back to him, "I would rather wait a year than publish a bad children's book, as I have too much respect for children."

E. B. White at The New Yorker, *1940s.*

But as time went on, the news of the war, the move back to New York, and his own writing made Andy anxious, nervous. He said his head felt as if there was "a kite caught in the branches somewhere," and "mice in the subconscious."

He described how he felt at a particularly low point: "I was almost sure I was about to die, my head felt so queer."

On the off chance that he *was* about to die, Andy wanted to finish his children's book so Katharine and Joel would have enough money to live on. Meanwhile, his editor had died. Just eight weeks after moving back to New York, Andy sent the finished manuscript of *Stuart Little* to his new editor at Harper and Brothers: Ursula Nordstrom.

Ursula wrote, "Only another children's book editor can know the emotions one has on hearing that a famous writer of adult books is going to send a book for children . . . for talent in the former does not always carry over to the latter." But she was relieved after she read Andy's manuscript. "I loved the diminutive hero, and I knew children would."

STUART LITTLE

When Mrs. Frederick C. Little's second son was born,
everybody noticed that it[he] was not much bigger than a mouse. The truth
of the matter was, the baby looked very much <u>like</u> a mouse in every way.
He was only about two inches high; and he had a mouse's sharp nose,
a mouse's tail, a mouse's whiskers, and the pleasant, shy manner of a
mouse. Before he was many days old he was not only looking like a
mouse but acting like one, too, -- wearing a grey hat and carrying
a small cane. Mr. and Mrs. Little named him Stuart, and Mr. Little
made him a tiny bed out of four clothes-pins and a cigarette box.

Unlike most babies, Stuart could walk as soon as
he was born. When he was a week old he could climb lamps by shinnying
up the cord. Mrs. Little saw right away that the infant clothes she
had provided were unsuitable, and she set to work and made him a fine
little blue worsted suit with patch pockets in which he could keep his
handkerchief, his money, and his keys. Every morning, before Stuart
dressed, Mrs. Little went into his room and weighed him on a small
scale which was really meant for weighing letters. At birth Stuart
could have been sent by first class mail for ~~two~~ three cents, but his
parents preferred to keep him rather than send him away; and when,
at the age of a month, he had gained only a third of an ounce, his
mother was so worried she sent for the doctor.

The doctor was delighted with Stuart, and said that
it was very unusual for an American family to have a mouse. He took
Stuart's temperature and found that it was 98.6, which is normal for a
mouse. He also examined Stuart's chest and heart and looked into his
ears solemnly with a tiny flashlight. [Not every doctor can [It is quite a thing to look into
a mouse's ear without laughing. Everything seemed to be all right, and
Mrs. Little was pleased to get such a good report. "Feed him up!" said

The first page of the manuscript of Stuart Little, *about 1944.*

Typically, the editor alone chooses the illustrator for a children's book, but Ursula included Andy in the search. They considered E. H. Shepard, the illustrator of *Winnie the Pooh*; they asked Robert Lawson, who had illustrated *The Story of Ferdinand*, but he was unavailable. Another five illustrators were rejected because their mice looked too much like Disney's Mickey Mouse. Finally, Andy suggested the artist Garth Williams, whose work he had seen when Garth was trying to sell cartoons to *The New Yorker*. Even though Garth had never illustrated a book before, his sketches for *Stuart Little* were just what Andy and Ursula had been hoping for.

wind

Schooner. The wind is abeam. The Wasp would look something this on the first leg of the race.

E. B. White sent Garth Williams pictures of schooners under sail for reference for the Wasp.

His note read:
"Schooner. The wind is abeam. The Wasp would look something [like] this on the first leg of the race."

After Andy saw Garth's final art for the book, he wrote, "I think Garth deserves all the bouquets that could be handed him for a brilliant and imaginative job. He has made the pictures enhance and add to the text in the way only the very best illustrators can and has made the book his book too in every way."

The publisher's catalog described Andy's novel this way: "Stuart Little is small in size only, has the adventurousness, the great purpose and the indomitable spirit of a classic figure, and his story [is] funny and tender and exciting by turns." Andy didn't like the word *classic*. No book was a classic before generations of readers proved it to be, he said. Andy claimed *Stuart Little* was just another book. To his distress, his publisher used the term anyway.

When the book was almost ready to go to press, Ursula sent Anne Carroll Moore a copy of the manuscript—everyone was eager to hear if *Stuart Little* would make the Library Lions roar. But Moore wrote a friend, "I was never so disappointed in a book in my life." She wrote an urgent fourteen-page letter to the Whites explaining why *Stuart Little*, with its "monstrous birth," should not be published. Not only was the story unfit for children and "out of hand," but White had blurred the line between fantasy and reality. How could a mouse be born to humans? "The two worlds are all mixed up," she wrote. "I fear *Stuart Little* will be very difficult to place in libraries and schools all over the country."

Katharine wrote a polite reply: "You are right of course that Stuart gets out of hand. . . . Didn't you think it even *funny*? . . . What I hope is that children of all ages will like *Stuart* for its humor. . . . It's a *dream*—quite literally—just as *Alice* is supposed to have been. Just recently the notes Andy made after he had that dream (more than twelve years ago) turned up, and I was surprised to find out how clearly the story followed them."

Stuart Little *cover by Garth Williams.*

A few days after *Stuart Little* came out, Andy's boss, Harold Ross, barged into his office. "Saw your book, White. You made one serious mistake!" Ross told him he should have said that Stuart was *adopted*, not *born*, to the Little family.

Maybe the worst criticism of all came from the librarian Frances Clarke Sayers, Moore's recent successor at the New York Public Library, who stamped on it NOT RECOMMENDED FOR PURCHASE BY EXPERT. Other libraries banned it too. E. B. White began to wonder if he had made a serious mistake. But what did the real experts think?

Letters from children started pouring in. Of the thousands Andy received, only two questioned how Stuart came into the world. Though many were uncertain about the ending, most loved the book.

March 11, 1946

Dear Mr. White:

We have just finished your book "Stuart Little." Our school librarian asked us to read it to help decide whether it would be a good book for the library. We think it would be, in fact, we think you stopped too soon. We'd like a continuation of the story. . . .

Sincerely yours,
THE SEVENTH GRADE

Children were proving *Stuart Little* to be a classic in the making.

FROM STUART LITTLE

DATE 1945

I N THE loveliest town of all, where the houses were white and high and the elm trees were green and higher than the houses, where the front yards were wide and pleasant and the back yards were bushy and worth finding out about, where the streets sloped down to the stream and the stream flowed quietly under the bridge, where the lawns ended in orchards and the orchards ended in fields and the fields ended in pastures and the pastures climbed the hill and disappeared over the top toward the wonderful wide sky, in this loveliest of all towns Stuart stopped to get a drink of sarsaparilla.

"It is unnerving to be told you're bad for children," Andy confessed. But he learned two things from writing *Stuart Little:* a writer's instinct is his best guide, and "children can sail easily over the fence that separates reality from make-believe. A fence that can throw a librarian is nothing to a child."

Later in the same year that the book came out, Ursula wrote to tell Andy that it had sold a hundred thousand copies. Andy gave her a jar of caviar—a gift of a hundred thousand sturgeon eggs.

In later editions of *Stuart Little*, E. B. White made one small change: the Littles' son was not born. Stuart *arrived*.

17 December

Dear Miss Nordstrom =

I feel
like the millionth person
through a turnstile —
dazed and happy. Dear
me, 100,000 books! It's
a little indecent, isn't it?

Yrs,
EBWhite

(over)

Letter to Ursula Nordstrom, 1947.

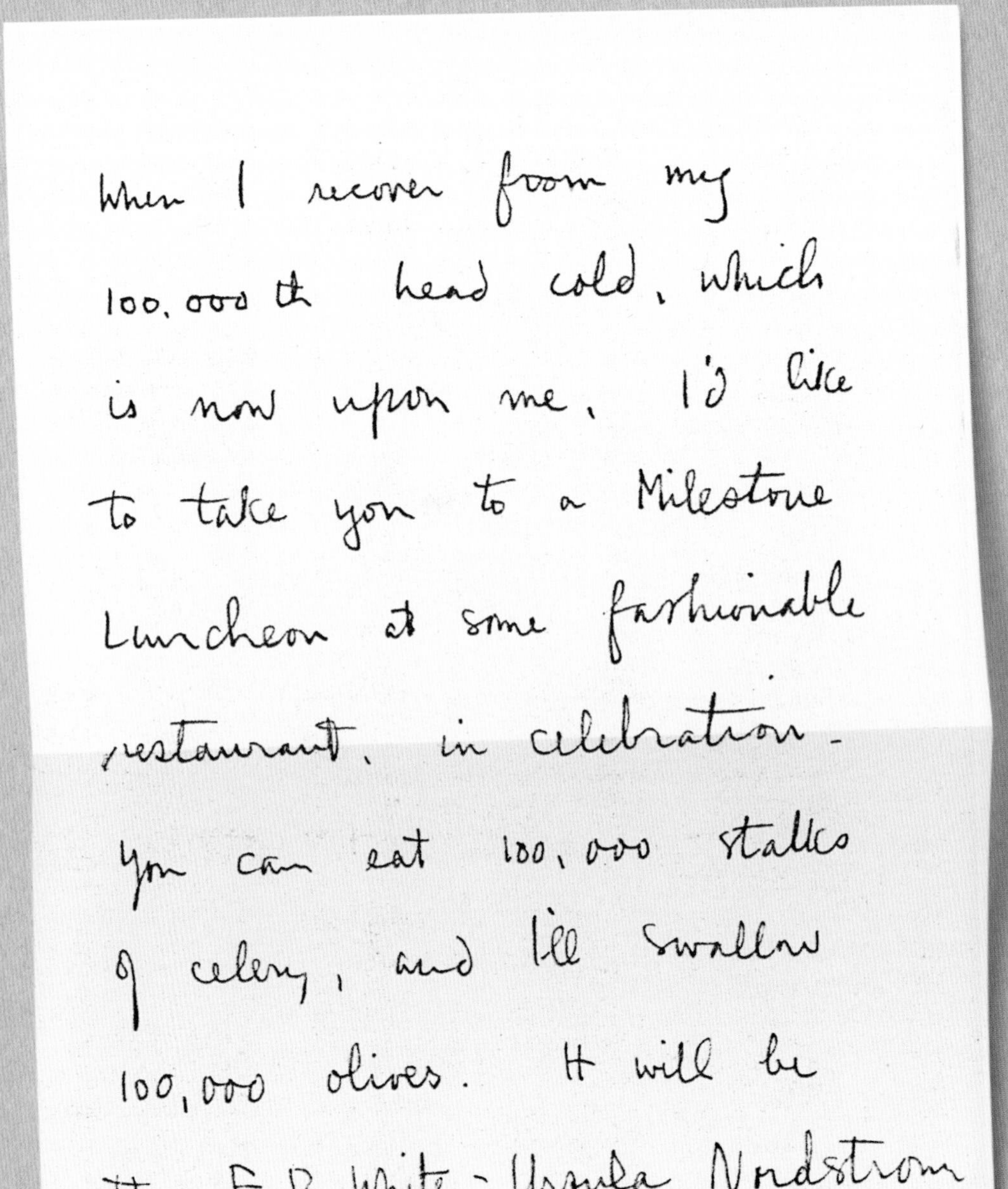

When I recover from my
100,000 th head cold, which
is now upon me, I'd like
to take you to a Milestone
Luncheon at some fashionable
restaurant, in celebration.
You can eat 100,000 stalks
of celery, and I'll swallow
100,000 olives. It will be
the E B White - Ursula Nordstrom
Book and Olive Luncheon.

EBW

Reverse side of letter to Ursula Nordstrom.

8

BAD NEWS

A pig shall be saved.

FRED WAS NOT Andy and Katharine's first dog, nor their last, but he was the dog Andy wrote most about. There was plenty to say about Fred.

Fred came from a pet store on Madison Avenue.[1] Though Andy considered Fred at times "vile," he could not imagine life without him.[2]

---

[1] "In no time at all, [Fred's] troubles cleared up and mine began," White wrote.

[2] "His activities and his character constitute an almost uninterrupted annoyance to me . . . Life without him would be heaven, but I am afraid it is not what I want."

One warm afternoon in Maine, Andy's pig failed to appear for supper. As Andy wrote, "When a pig (or a child) refuses supper a chill wave of fear runs through any household." As it became evident the pig was not well, Andy worried.

The animals on the White farm were part of a natural rhythm. They were born, nursed, and fed, and they enjoyed peaceful surroundings. And then (some) swiftly died. Raising animals to be butchered sometimes bothered Andy. "I do not like to betray a person or a creature," he said. After befriending his animals, this felt like "double-dealing." But, like most who raise animals, he farmed for food. Still, even if this sick pig was meant for slaughter, he didn't like seeing it suffer.

Andy called neighbors for advice. He and Joel tried giving the pig castor oil, then an enema. As the pig worsened, Fred's spirits seemed to rise.[3] Eventually a vet arrived and repeated what Andy had done, but still the pig's health declined. By now the pig did not even have the strength to make a bed for himself. Andy went to tend to the pig one last evening and saw with grief that the pig had died.

Andy went to bed. When he awoke the next morning, his handyman, Lennie, was already digging the grave. Fred was

---

[3] "[Fred] was an notorious ghoul," White wrote.

KNELT, SAW that he was dead, and left him there: his face had a mild look, expressive neither of deep peace nor of deep suffering, although I think he had suffered a good deal.

FROM ATLANTIC MONTHLY
TITLE "Death of a Pig"
DATE 1948

"supervising."[4] Under a bleak gray sky, Lennie and Andy hauled the pig into the grave and filled it with dirt. Andy tied a rope to Fred, and they all made their way back to the house, Fred reluctantly bringing up the rear.[5]

Though death was part of life on the farm, the death of the pig unsettled Andy. He looked for redemption—he wanted to find some way to save a pig's life.

When Fred died later that year, at age thirteen, Andy buried him near the pig—and decided to write a book about animals and about saving a pig's life. But by what miracle on a farm could a pig's life be saved? Andy began to be on the lookout for wonders.

---

[4] "Fred patrolled the brink in simple but impressive circles."
[5] "The grave in the woods is unmarked, but Fred can direct the mourner to it unerringly and with immense good will.

[F̲R̲E̲D̲'̲S̲] GRAVE IS the only grave I visit with any
regularity...I do not experience grief when I am
down there....But I feel sadness at All Last Things...
sorrow not at my dog's death, but at my own, which
hasn't even occurred yet but which saddens me just
to think about in such pleasant surroundings.

FROM	ESSAYS OF E.B. WHITE
TITLE	"Bedfellows"
DATE	1956

9

CHARLOTTE'S WEB

I had as much trouble getting off the ground as
the Wright Brothers.

ONE OCTOBER EVENING Andy watched a spider spin
an egg sac and deposit her eggs. A few days later,
he carefully detached the egg sac, put it in an old candy box
with air holes, and brought it with him back to New York.
He left it on his dresser, and a few weeks later he noticed
hundreds of tiny spiders coming out of the air holes and
stringing lines from the box to his mirror, his comb, his
brush. An entomologist from the Museum of Natural History
helped him identify the spider as *Aranea cavatica*, "a plain
grey spider that prefers shady situations. It lives in houses

and barns in northern New England. Its webs are sometimes very large."

Later, back in Maine, as Andy was bringing a pail of slops to the barn, an idea struck him: He wanted to write a story about animals . . . he needed a way to save a pig's life . . . *could a spider save a pig?* He wrote to his editor Ursula to ask if there had ever been a spider as a main character in a children's book. Not as far as she knew, she said, or at least not since Miss Muffet.

In October 1949, he wrote his publisher, Cass Canfield: "My next book *is* in sight. I look at it every day. I keep it in a carton, as you would a kitten." Andy spent the year studying spiders. "In this," he wrote, "I found the key to the story." Andy would not make his heroine, Charlotte A. Cavatica, conform to his narrative; his story would have to adapt to how spiders behave. For example, Andy learned that some male species of spiders "dance," so in one draft, Charlotte tells Wilbur, the pig, that her husband was "some dancer." When Fern listens as Charlotte tells the barn animals how her cousin cast a web that caught a fish, Andy was being true to spiders because in rare cases spiders have caught small birds and fish. And when Wilbur takes Charlotte's egg sac to the farm in his mouth, it makes sense because *A. cavatica*'s egg sacs are waterproof.

WISH YOU COULD be here today to see my characters in the flesh. Had a lamb arrive yesterday morning at breakfast time - a boy. He is already out in the barnyard, playing in a snowdrift. Two of my geese are nesting - one of them right in the sheepshed, the other atop a manure pile. Charlotte's children are due shortly. It's quite a day here today.

FROM LETTERS OF E.B. WHITE

DATE 1952

claws

tarsus

metatars

tibia

patella

of

book lung

furrow

spiracle

ts

ted.

A

A. Do

When Andy finished the story in 1951, he wrote to Ursula that a draft was complete but he wasn't quite satisfied with it, so he had set it aside to let it "ripen." Months later, though the tale still featured the barn and its animals, Andy had added five more chapters to give Fern more importance in the story.

And he kept struggling with the first line. He began:

Charlotte was a grey spider who lived in the doorway of a barn.

Then he tried:

I shall speak first of Wilbur.

Then:

A barn can have a horse in it, and a barn can have a cow in it, and a barn can have hens scratching in the chaff and swallows flying in and out through the door—but if a barn hasn't got a pig in it, it is hardly worth talking about.

After setting aside the story for a year, he tried:

At midnight, John Arable pulled his boots on, lit a lantern, and walked out to the hoghouse.

Last, White cut to the action and tried: "Where's Papa going with that hand ax?," then shortening it to:

"Where's Papa going with that ax?"

and plenty of tricks
up her sleeve.

I.

She was about the size of a gumdrop, and she had eight legs, ~~which is enough for any one.~~

Charlotte was a ~~big~~ / grey spider who lived in the doorway of a barn. / But there is no use talking about Charlotte until we have looked into the matter of the barn. This barn was large. It was old. It was white. *painted* It smelled of hay and it smelled of manure. It was pleasantly warm in winter, pleasantly cool in summer; it had stalls for horses, *the work* tie-ups for the ~~cows~~ cows, an ~~scaffold~~ loft, *up above* for the hay ~~there chilled old juices and roll~~ *underneath* a place down ~~below~~ for sheep. a ~~place~~ *pen* ~~down below~~ for a pig, a grain bin, a rat trap, a lot of sunlight coming in through the ~~big~~ doors, *on sunny days, a lot of* and it *rain beating against the* ~~east windows on rainy days.~~ *east windows on rainy days.* was owned by a fellow named Zuckerman. ~~Of all ~~Zuckerman was proud of his barn. He was always~~~~ *barn of Zuckerman's* Of all the barns I ever saw, ~~this~~ was *Charlotte, the spider, must have thought so, too, or* the most agreeable. ~~There was always~~ something going on she never would have built her web in the doorway, ~~& she picked an awfully good doorway~~ *the* ~~very carefully~~ ~~thing, & she didn't the web was~~ When I say doorway I don't mean the *big* main doorway where the horses ~~got~~ went in and out, and I don't mean the

Chapter I. ESCAPE.

I shall speak first of Wilbur.

Wilbur was a small, ~~beautifully~~ ~~nicely~~ ~~behaved~~ ~~symmetrical~~ pig living in a manure pile in the cellar of a barn. ~~He was~~ what farmers call a spring pig — which simply means that he ~~offered~~ was ~~to be~~ born in springtime. But there is no use talking about Wilbur until we have looked into the matter of the barn itself — The barn was very large. It was very old. ~~It~~ It smelled of hay and it smelled of manure — It smelled of the perspiration of tired horses and the ~~wonderful~~ ~~sweet~~ breath of patient cows — It smelled of grain and of harness dressing and of axle grease and of rubber boots and of new rope. And whenever the cat was given a fish-head to eat, the barn would smell of fish — But mostly it smelled of hay, for there was always hay in the great loft up overhead. And there was always hay being pitched down to the cows and the horses. The barn was pleasantly warm in winter when the animals spent most of their time indoors; and it was pleasantly cool in summer when the big doors stood wide open to the breeze. It had stalls, on the main floor for the ~~heavy~~ work horses, ~~it~~ ~~had~~ tie-ups, on the main floor ~~so~~ ~~stanchions~~ for the cows; a pen down underneath for the sheep, a place, down underneath for Wilbur ~~the pig~~, ~~a grain bin~~, and it was full of all sorts of ~~equipment~~ things that you ordinarily find in barns — ladders, grindstones, hay forks, monkey wrenches,

It often had a sort of peaceful smell — as though nothing bad could ever happen ever again in the world.

Another draft with Wilbur the pig beginning the story.

CHARLOTTE

Chapter I.   The Barn

A barn can have a horse in it, and
a barn can have a cow in it, and a barn
can have hens scratching in the chaff
and swallows flying in and out through
the door — but if a barn hasn't got
a pig in it, it is hardly worth
talking about.   I am very glad to say that Mr.
Zuckerman's barn had a pig in it, and therefore I
feel free to talk about ~~it as much as~~ want to.   The pig's

~~....~~
~~Zuckerman's barn ... that it was built on the~~
~~....~~   ~~....~~

name was Wilbur. He was small and white, except when
he was dirty ~~and then~~ then he was small and brown.
Wilbur did not get dirty on purpose, but he lived in the ~~a~~
lower part of the barn ~~underneath the where the cows were.~~
~~It~~ where

Another first page draft of Charlotte's Web, beginning with a description of the barn leading into the introduction of Wilbur. Note White's drawing of Charlotte in the upper left corner.

Chapter I
MIDNIGHT

At midnight, John Arable pulled his boots on, lit
a lantern, and walked out to the hoghouse. The sky was clear and the earth
smelled of springtime. Inside the hoghouse, the old sow lay on her side;
her eyes were closed. Huddled in a corner stood the newborn pigs, eleven
of them. They had their heads together, in a circle, like football players
before a play. Mr. Arable set his lantern down, leaned on the rail, and
smiled. Then he began counting. "One, two, three, four..."

"Eleven," he said at last. "Ten good ones and one
little runty pig. Funny there's always one that's smaller than the others."

Then he thought to himself: "Well, no matter---the
sow can only take care of ten, anyway. I'll get rid of the runt in the
morning."

He waited a few minutes to see that everything was
all right with the new family, then he walked back to the house, blew his
lantern out, undressed, and climbed into bed.

"Did the pigs come?" asked his wife, sleepily.

"Yes, eleven of them," said Mr. Arable.

"Can that sow feed eleven?" asked Mrs. Arable.

"No. She can feed ten."

"What'll you do with the eleventh pig?"

*After setting the story aside for a year, White begins this draft with the Arable family and places the animals
in the background.*

table for breakfast.

"Where's Papa going with that ax?" said Fern to
her mother ~~as they were having breakfast.~~ *as* They were ~~in sitting in~~ *setting the*
~~the kitchen having breakfast.~~ *the kitchen*

"Out to the hoghouse," replied Mrs. Arable. "Some
pigs were born last night."

"I don't see why he needs an ax," continued Fern,
who was only eight~~, years old.~~

"Well," said her mother, ~~typexofxthexpigx~~ "eleven
~~pigs were born~~, and one of ~~them~~ *the pig* is a runt~~x just a little bit of a~~ *It's very small, and*
~~thing.~~ *doesn't amount to much.* Your father will have to do away with it. It's no good." ~~Knock it on the head~~

"Do away with it?" shrieked Fern, "You mean __kill__
it? Just because it's smaller than the others?"

Mrs. Arable ~~helpedxherselfx~~ put her spoon down
on her plate. "Don't yell, Fern!" she said. "Your father is
~~doing what is~~ right. The pig would probably die anyway."

Fern slid out of her chair, and ran outdoors~~/ to the~~ *down*
~~xxxtchingxupxwithxherxfather~~ *The grass was wet and the earth smelled*
~~justxasxfastxasxshexcouldxgoxxxThexgrassxwasxwetxwithxdew~~ *of springtime.*
~~chase of springtime.~~ ~~of x~~
~~xxxtchxupxwithxher father.~~ ~~The grass was wet with dew and her~~
Fern sneakers were ~~xxxx sopping wet before~~ *by the time* she caught up with ~~him.~~ *her father.*

"Please don't kill it!" she sobbed. "It's unfair.'"

Mr. Arable stopped walking.

"Fern," *he* said ~~her father,~~ gently, "you will have to
learn to control yourself."

"Control myself?" yelled Fern. "This is a matter

After revising for another year, Andy sent the final manuscript to Ursula. She loved it immediately, and did not recommend changing a word. But after she saw a printer's proof, she wrote to Katharine urging the Whites to consider

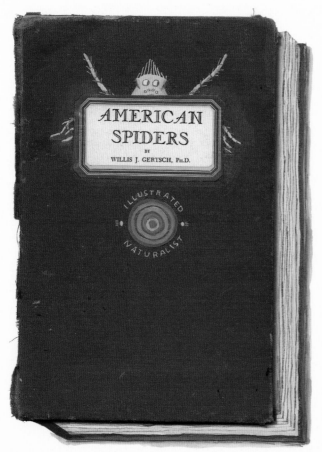

one important alteration: changing the title of the second-to-last chapter from "The Death of Charlotte" to "Last Day," so as not to give away the ending.

Garth Williams agreed to illustrate *Charlotte's Web,* describing the story as "just perfect." Andy wanted Charlotte's character to be both "beguiling" and "a New Englander, precise and disciplined." Garth based Fern on his daughter Fiona, but he struggled with drawing Charlotte.

He tried putting a human face on Charlotte. That was not the look Andy was after. Andy then sent Garth two spider books for reference (Garth later described them as "gruesome").

THERE IS A very funny picture in this book that I think Garth should see. It is "A"...The eyes and hair are quite fetching.

Plate I shows an orb web covered with dew.

FROM LETTERS OF E.B. WHITE

DATE 1952

PLATE I

Richard L. Cassell

Orb web covered with dew

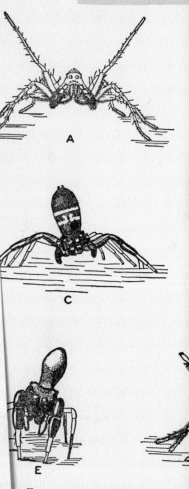

A

C

E

XT FIG. 2.—COURTSHIP POSTUR
JUMPING SPI
a *milvina* Hentz. B. *Habronattus vi*
z. D. *Hyctia pikei* Peckham. E.
Euophrys monadnock
(Redrawn from Kaston, Emer

Above left: *Garth Williams's sketches begin with human faces.*

Above: *His later rendering, inspired by the Mona Lisa.*

Left: *The final drawing of Charlotte as she appears in* Charlotte's Web. *Of the final drawing Garth wrote, "White accepted the accurate rendition of the Aranea cavatica." Note White's three hairs and two tiny eyes looking downward added to Charlotte's face.*

Garth wrote, "I struggled to invent a loveable spider-face.... Finally I gave her a Mona Lisa face, as she is, after all, the heroine of the story.

Many sketches later, Garth had her *almost* perfectly rendered when Andy added two eyes and three hairs to Garth's drawing. Now she was pretty *and* a New Englander.

Charlotte's Web was finally released in 1952.

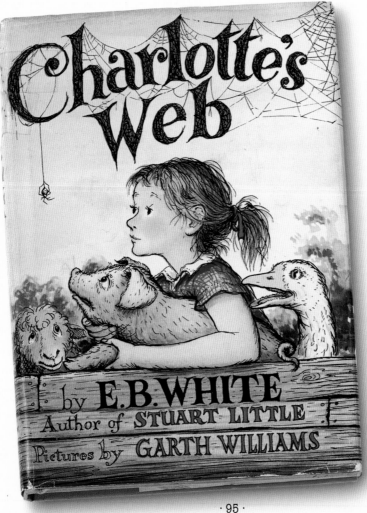

Charlotte's Web
cover by Garth Williams.

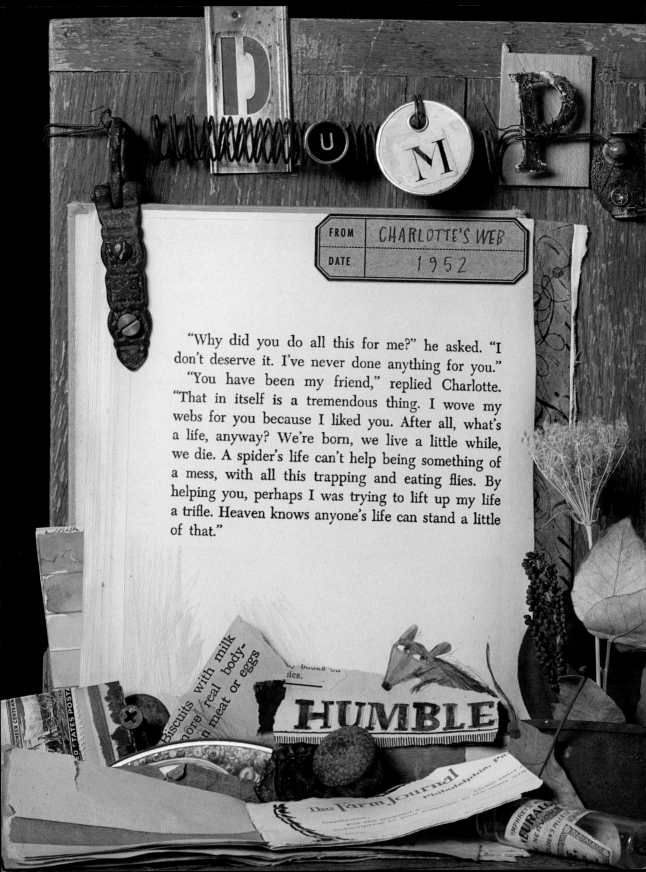

FROM CHARLOTTE'S WEB
DATE 1952

"Why did you do all this for me?" he asked. "I don't deserve it. I've never done anything for you."

"You have been my friend," replied Charlotte. "That in itself is a tremendous thing. I wove my webs for you because I liked you. After all, what's a life, anyway? We're born, we live a little while, we die. A spider's life can't help being something of a mess, with all this trapping and eating flies. By helping you, perhaps I was trying to lift up my life a trifle. Heaven knows anyone's life can stand a little of that."

In one review, the writer Eudora Welty describes the story: "What the book is about is friendship on earth, affection and protection, adventure and miracle, life and death, trust and treachery, pleasure and pain, and the passing of time. . . . What it all proves . . . is that human beings must always be on the watch for the coming of wonders. . . . As a piece of work it is just about perfect."

Though Andy agreed to allow a movie to be made, he was skeptical that the magic of the story could be captured on film. He reminded the movie's director that "the film should be a paean to life, a hymn to the barn, an acceptance of dung. The barn is a community of rugged individualists, everybody mildly suspicious of everybody else, including me." He went to great lengths to ensure that the movie was as close to the book as possible, that "Templeton starts as a rat and ends as a rat," and, most important, that Charlotte dies.

Charlotte's Web won a Newbery Honor and remains one of the most beloved children's books of all time. When Andy recorded the audiobook for *Charlotte's Web*, it took him seventeen takes to get through "Last Day," the chapter in which Charlotte dies. "It's ridiculous," he told the producer, "a grown man reading a book that he wrote, and being unable to read it aloud because of tears."

JUST WANT to add that there is no symbolism
in "Charlotte's Web." And there is no political
meaning in the story. It is a straight report
from the barn cellar, which I dearly love, having
spent so many fine hours there, winter and summer,
spring and fall, good times and bad times, with
garrulous geese, the passage of swallows, the
nearness of rats, and the sameness of sheep.

FROM **LETTERS OF E.B. WHITE**
DATE 1971

THE ELEMENTS OF STYLE

A misspelled word is an abomination.

IN MAINE, Andy wrote in his boathouse, which was the same size and dimensions as the cabin where Henry David Thoreau wrote *Walden*. Inside the boathouse were the same things Thoreau had had in his cabin: a table, a chair, a wood stove. Andy wrote, "*Walden* is the only book I own, although there are some others unclaimed on my shelves." Thoreau's cry of "simplicity, simplicity, simplicity" had for Andy "the insistence of a fire alarm" and inspired not only his writing but how he lived his life.

One day, a Cornell classmate sent Andy *The Elements of Style*, a book written by his old English professor Will Strunk. Andy had forgotten the book, but not his professor. (Will Strunk had died a few years earlier.) Almost immediately, Andy wrote an essay for *The New Yorker* describing Strunk and his "little book" on the fundamentals of English grammar that urged writing students to be "clear, brief, bold." An editor at Macmillan, Jack Case, read the essay and wanted to publish a revised *Elements of Style* by Strunk *and* White, with Andy's essay as an introduction. Andy agreed, concluding the book with "An Approach to Style," which was advice based on what he had learned as a writer.

Professor Will Strunk, Jr.

OMIT
NEEDLESS WORDS

"**V**igorous writing is concise. A sentence should contain no unnecessary words, a paragraph no unnecessary sentences, for the same reason that a drawing should have no unnecessary lines and a machine no unnecessary parts. This requires not that the writer make all his sentences short, or that he avoid all detail and treat his subjects only in outline, but that every word tell."

THERE YOU have a short, valuable essay on the nature and beauty of brevity—sixty-three words that could change the world.

FROM	THE ELEMENTS OF STYLE
DATE	1959

The book began with rules of grammar:

> *Form the possessive singular of nouns by adding 's. Follow this rule whatever the final consonant. Thus write,*
>> *Charles's friend.*
>> *Burns's poems*
>> *The witch's malice*

Then the book moved on to rules of composition:

> *Writing, to be effective, must follow closely the thoughts of the writer, but not necessarily in the order in which those thoughts occur.*

And form:

> ***Exclamations.** Do not attempt to emphasize simple statements by using a mark of exclamation.*
>> *It was a wonderful show! It was a wonderful show.*
>
> *The exclamation mark is to be reserved for use after true exclamations or commands.*
>> *What a wonderful show!*
>> *Halt!*

And commonly misused words and expressions:

> ***Like.** Not to be used for the conjunction* as.
>> *We spent the evening like We spent the evening as*
>> *in the old days. in the old days.*

But once a writer understands the rules of grammar, what about *style?* In *The Elements of Style*, White writes, "The approach to style is by way of plainness, simplicity, orderliness, sincerity." He offers hints for the beginning writer. More than a few good writers have taken his suggestions.

The poet Joyce Sidman, a Newbery honoree, writes, "White's points in his 'List of Reminders' are the fundamentals on which I have built my own writing style. 'Be clear' but 'Do not explain too much' and 'Write with nouns and verbs' would be, indeed, the recipe for good poetry.

"I still use *The Elements of Style* to look up the lingering question *That* or *which*?"

That. Which. That *is the defining, or restrictive, pronoun;* which *the nondefining or nonrestrictive.*
The lawn mower that is broken is in the garage.
(Tells which one.)
The lawn mower, which is broken, is in the garage.
(Adds a fact about the only mower in question.)

White's early poem "A Story of a Little Mouse" (see page 20) is an example of the proper use of the word "which," as is Sidman's "that" in her following poem, "Bat Wraps Up."

Bat Wraps Up

Belly full,
he drops down
from the echoing room of night.
One last swift swoop,
one last bug plucked from air
with cupped tail,
scooped neatly to mouth.

As dark grows thin
and body heavy,
he tumbles to tree
and grasps bark,
folds that swirl of cape
tipped with tiny claws
and snags the spot
that smells like home.

Then . . . upside flip,
lock-on grip . . .
stretch, hang, relax.
Yawn . . .
        dawn.

—Joyce Sidman,
from *Dark Emperor
and Other Poems
of the Night*

Paul Fleischman, a Newbery medalist, writes, "I have this rule carved deep in memory . . .

Avoid the use of qualifiers.
Rather, very, little, pretty—these are the leeches that
infest the pond of prose, sucking the blood of words.

"I actually once tried to write an entire novel without a single adverb. I didn't quite make it—sometimes you need them—but sentences are almost always stronger without them. I could have begun *Seedfolks* with 'Hesitantly, I stood barefoot a few feet in front of our extremely old, chipped mahogany altar.' But less is often more in writing, which is why the opening sentences read, 'I stood before our family altar. It was dawn. No one else in the apartment was awake.'"

Kate DiCamillo, also a Newbery medalist, writes, "Though I have the *Elements of Style* within two steps of my desk (and refer to it frequently), what I keep going back to in a ritualistic way are White's essays, and *Charlotte's Web*, of course. The thing about White that comforts and fascinates me (and challenges me) is how he manages to make his words matter more. It is as if he is able to make one word do the work of ten. He bears down with the whole of his heart and soul on each word he chooses."

For those trying to find the right words and to edit their own work, E. B. White suggested that "revising is part of writing" and that if writing needs "stirring up, scissors should be brought into play."

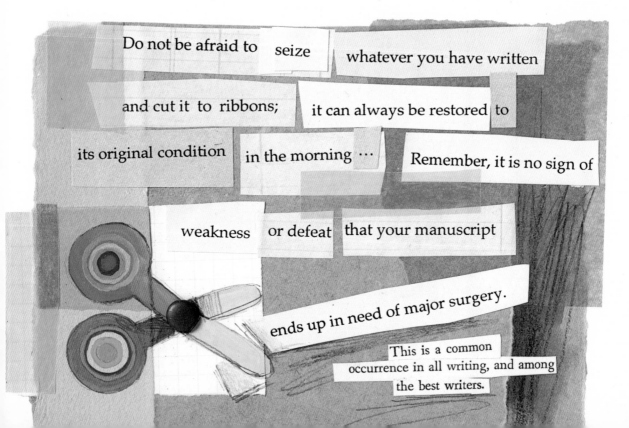

Do not be afraid to seize whatever you have written and cut it to ribbons; it can always be restored to its original condition in the morning ⋯ Remember, it is no sign of weakness or defeat that your manuscript ends up in need of major surgery. This is a common occurrence in all writing, and among the best writers.

Even though Andy had agreed to work on the revised edition of *The Elements of Style* (under the condition that it stayed true to Strunk's original text) he did not consider himself a grammarian. "When I finally can't take any more grammar," he wrote, "I hop on my bicycle and go scorching up and down the highway to remove the cobwebs." He wrote to his editor Jack Case, "I feel a terrible responsibility in this project and it is making me jumpy." Three years after the revised edition was published, Andy wrote to Case:

Fiddler Bayou
30 March [1962]

Dear Jack,
The next grammar book I bring out I want to tell how to end a sentence with five prepositions. A father of a little boy goes upstairs after supper to read to his son, but he brings the wrong book. The boy says, "What did you bring that book that I don't want to be read to out of up for?"
And how are YOU?

Yrs, Andy

11

THE TRUMPET OF THE SWAN

In almost everyone's life there is one event
that changes the whole course of his existence.

BY THE FALL OF 1968, Katharine was in poor health. Medical bills began piling up. Andy needed money. Even though *Charlotte's Web* had sold very well, when Andy signed the contract, he'd agreed to take only a portion of the sales each year; the rest of the earnings were being held by the publisher. ("Probably in a sock somewhere," he said.) He decided to write another children's book.

An article in the *New York Times* about trumpeter swans gave Andy an idea for a story about a trumpeter swan born without a voice. Andy named the character Louis, after the jazz trumpeter Louis Armstrong. He later wrote a young reader that, like the young swan Louis, he "needed money."

Andy had never seen or heard a trumpeter swan, but he learned there was a swan family living on Bird Lake at the Philadelphia Zoo. Since Philly was the home of his old friend Cush (who called Andy "Ho" and himself "Hum"), in October of 1968, Andy wrote him a letter.

> *Dear Cush:*
>
> *How would you like to do some sleuthing for an aging fiction writer? I've never visited the Zoo . . . What does Bird Lake look like? Is it pleasing, ugly, small, big, what? . . .*
>
> *Are there any Trumpeter Swans in residence today? How many? . . .*
>
> *And now a sudden switch. Night clubs! In what general area of Philadelphia would one find a night spot? . . .*
>
> *So go forth, Old Friend. Case the Gardens for me. Tell me how they smell, what they look like. Examine the swans on Bird Lake. . . .*
>
> *Love, Ho*
>
> *P.S. To prepare yourself for this preposterous task, you should probably bone up on nomenclature. A male swan is a cob. A female is a pen. A baby swan is a cygnet. (But don't say I told you.)*

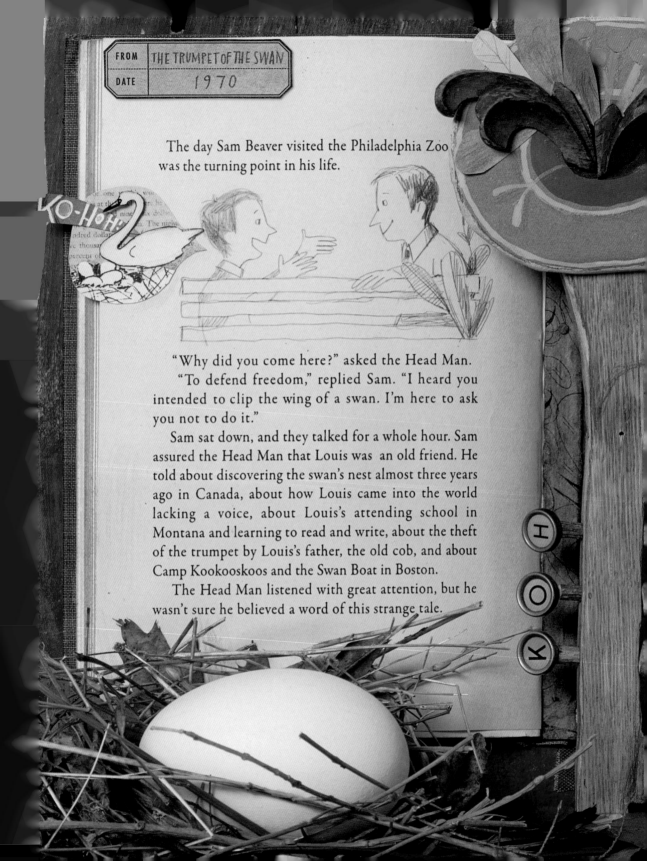

The day Sam Beaver visited the Philadelphia Zoo was the turning point in his life.

KO-HOH!

"Why did you come here?" asked the Head Man.

"To defend freedom," replied Sam. "I heard you intended to clip the wing of a swan. I'm here to ask you not to do it."

Sam sat down, and they talked for a whole hour. Sam assured the Head Man that Louis was an old friend. He told about discovering the swan's nest almost three years ago in Canada, about how Louis came into the world lacking a voice, about Louis's attending school in Montana and learning to read and write, about the theft of the trumpet by Louis's father, the old cob, and about Camp Kookooskoos and the Swan Boat in Boston.

The Head Man listened with great attention, but he wasn't sure he believed a word of this strange tale.

Ursula did like the story, and both she and Andy hoped Garth Williams would illustrate it. But Garth was living in Mexico and was too far away to create the art in time. Everyone was disappointed. When Andy heard the news, he wrote to Garth Williams, "I am very sad tonight . . . I'm not entirely happy with the text of the book—I am old and wordy and the book seems to show it." Eventually, they chose the artist Edward Frascino. Meanwhile, Andy had an idea for a book cover. Not being an artist himself, he asked his neighbor Dorothy B. Hayes to do a watercolor sketch of a trumpeter swan pulling on a boy's shoelace. Andy gave her sketch to Frascino, who repainted the concept for the cover.

When Andy's new book was released in 1970, everyone was eager to read it.

A portion of the watercolor sketch for The Trumpet of the Swan *by Andy's friend and neighbor, Dorothy B. Hayes, 1970.*

Before long, Cush sent Andy the results of his research and some photographs. Andy wrote back to Cush, "The snapshots from Bird Lake are an inspiration to me and I am encouraged to go on."

Andy did more research from Maine. In his story, the young cygnet Louis stays at the Ritz Hotel and orders twelve watercress sandwiches from room service. What would that have cost? Andy called a friend who worked near the Ritz to find out.

Unlike what he'd done with his other two children's books, Andy did not set this story aside to see if it needed changes.

November 17, 1969

Dear Ursula:

This morning I sent off the manuscript to you by registered mail. It is called "The Trumpet of the Swan" and it is about a cygnet that has a speech defect—along with other problems, including a money problem.

If you think the book is promising, let me know, and if you think it's lousy, I would like to know that, too. The Trumpeter Swan, largest of the American waterfowl, was once almost extinct but has made a comeback. This book is about a young Trumpeter.

Yrs,
Andy

Watercolor print of a trumpeter swan by John James Audubon.

U.S. DEPARTMENT OF THE INTERIOR
VOID AFTER JUNE 30,1951

$2 MIGRATORY BIRD HUNTING STAMP

Keeokuskh, *kee-o-kusk'*, the muskrat.
Keeonekh, *kee'o-nek*, the otter..
Killooleet, *kil'loo-leet*, the white-throated sparrow.
Kookooskoos, *koo-koo-skoos'*, the great horned owl.
Koskomenos, *kŏs'kŏm-e-nŏs'*, the kingfisher.
Kupkawis, *cup-ka'wis*, the barred owl.
Kwaseekho, *kwá-seek'ho*, the sheldrake.

The reviews for *Trumpet of the Swan* came in strong. When a group of young students wrote to Andy to ask about the violence in the book, he wrote back, "I go by my instinct. I write largely for myself and am content to believe

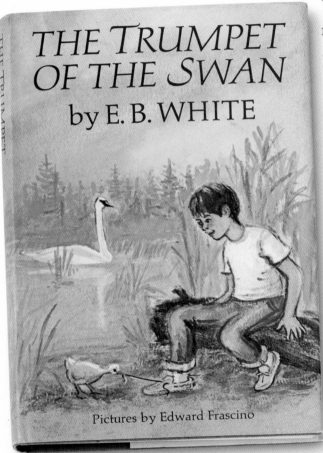

what is good enough for me is good enough for a youngster . . . 'Charlotte' was a story of friendship, life, death, salvation. 'Stuart Little' was a story of a quest—the quest for beauty." *This* story, he later wrote, was a love story. Not just the love between Louis and his new wife, Serena, but between fathers and sons—Sam Beaver and his dad, Louis and the old cob. Andy even noted at one point that the old cob spoke to Louis in the

The Trumpet of the Swan cover by Edward Frascino.

unmistakable voice of Andy's own father, Samuel White. Andy wrote, "Father was quite a talker and didn't hesitate to say in twenty words what could be said in six."

WELCOME TO THE pond and the swamp adjacent!...
Welcome to the world that contains this lonely
pond, this splendid marsh, unspoiled and wild!
Welcome to sunlight and shadow, wind and weather;
welcome to water!...Welcome to danger, which you
must guard against - the vile fox...the offensive
otter...the stinking skunk. Beware of lead pellets
that lie on the bottom of all ponds, left there
by the guns of hunters. Don't eat them - they'll
poison you! Be vigilant, be strong, be brave,
be graceful, and always follow me!

FROM THE TRUMPET OF THE SWAN
DATE 1970

In his review of *The Trumpet of the Swan*, the author John Updike wrote:

> The world of E. B. White's children's books is eminently a reasonable one. . . . When . . . the director of Camp Kookooskoos is sprayed by a skunk . . . he announces that the camp has been given "a delicious dash of wild perfume." . . . Similarly, in "Stuart Little," when a mouse instead of a baby is born to human parents, they promptly improvise for him a "tiny bed out of four clothespins and a cigarette box." When, in "Charlotte's Web," the pig squeals "I don't want to die!" the spider says, "I can't stand hysterics."
>
> "The Trumpet of the Swan" glows with the primal ecstasies of space and flight, of night and day, of nurturing and maturing, of courtship and art. On the last page Louis thinks of "how lucky he was to inhabit such a beautiful earth, how lucky he had been to solve his problems with music." How rare that word "lucky" has become! The universe remains chancy, but no one admits to having good luck. We, and our children, are lucky to have this book.

Later, the Philadelphia Orchestra set *The Trumpet of the Swan* to music. "Imagine me," wrote White, "sitting down there in my boathouse a year and a half ago, composing the lines of Sam Beaver's poem and not having the slightest inkling that the Philadelphia Orchestra was tuning up onstage. What a life I lead! How merry! How innocent! How nutty!"

SAM BEAVER'S POEM

Of all the places on land and sea,
Philadelphia's zoo is the place for me.
There's plenty to eat and a lot to do,
There's a Frigate Bird and a tiny Shrew,
There's a Vesper Rat and a Two-toed Sloth,
And it's fair to say that I like them both...
The houses are clean, the keepers are kind,
And one baboon has a pink behind....

FROM	THE TRUMPET OF THE SWAN
DATE	1970

WHAT DO OUR HEARTS TREASURE?

Old age is a special problem for me because I've never been able to shed the mental image I have of myself - a lad of about nineteen.

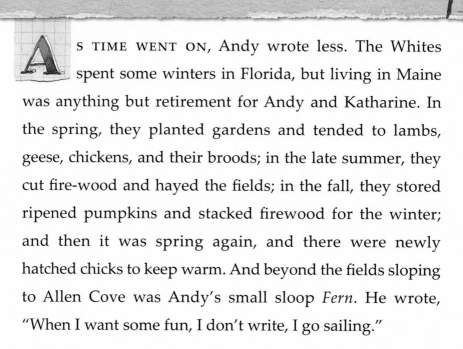

A S TIME WENT ON, Andy wrote less. The Whites spent some winters in Florida, but living in Maine was anything but retirement for Andy and Katharine. In the spring, they planted gardens and tended to lambs, geese, chickens, and their broods; in the late summer, they cut fire-wood and hayed the fields; in the fall, they stored ripened pumpkins and stacked firewood for the winter; and then it was spring again, and there were newly hatched chicks to keep warm. And beyond the fields sloping to Allen Cove was Andy's small sloop *Fern*. He wrote, "When I want some fun, I don't write, I go sailing."

Andy and Katharine on their farm in Maine.

Joel now lived nearby with his own family. Andy once wrote that Joel's boat *Flounder* had "launched a thousand ships." Joel had become a naval architect and ran a boatyard, designing and building traditional wooden boats. He built boats with the same verve Andy brought to writing. Joel designed and built his dad a twenty-foot sloop that he named *Martha* (after Andy's granddaughter), and he rigged it so Andy could sail it alone.

In 1977, after a series of illnesses, Katharine died of heart failure. At her service, the family read Andy's poem "Natural History" (see page 47). Andy did not go; he was too distraught. Later, Andy planted an oak tree at her gravesite. He wrote a friend, "I have lost the one thing that seemed to make any sense in my life, and I feel like a child lost at Coney Island."

Life did go on. He spent his time doing chores around the barn, sailing, and playing with his grandchildren. Andy and *New Yorker* editor Dorothy Lobrano Guth finished a project he and Katharine had begun—editing the tens of thousands of letters he had written over his lifetime for a new book: *Letters of E. B. White*. That collection was as close to an autobiography as Andy would get.

In time, Andy gave up sailing, but not boating. For his eighty-first birthday, he borrowed a canoe and went back to Belgrade Lakes. He wrote, "The trip was a success, the

The photographer Jill Krementz took this photo of E. B. White and Joel White in front of Joel's Brooklin Boat Yard, August 18, 1976, in Center Harbor, Maine.

weather smiled, and the canoe, which leaked only slightly, could have been called *Summer Memories*." When he returned home, he bought himself an Old Town canoe, just like the one his dad had given him for his eleventh birthday.

He later wrote to a friend, "The year is only a few days old but I am already in my thoughts careening toward summer and fall, awaiting the day when I can boost my canoe on top of the car and set out for the lake."

'LL BE 85 in July. Am still riding a bike but have lost the sight in one eye, along with a lot of other losses. Last fall I was tooling along on my 3-speed Raleigh when a coyote emerged from the woods and followed me. I don't think he was anything but curious, but it was kind of spooky to have a wild animal tailing me. I was probably his first octogenarian on wheels and he just wanted to get a good look at it.

FROM LETTERS OF E.B. WHITE

DATE 1984

Because his eyesight was failing, Andy resigned from writing Newsbreaks for *The New Yorker* in 1982. (He had written more than 30,000 Newsbreaks.) Andy thanked William Shawn and the magazine for keeping him "gainfully employed over such a long period of time."

One day, after Andy went canoeing, he stumbled and hit his head. Later on, he complained he wasn't feeling right. He was never quite himself again. Doctors diagnosed him with dementia. Eventually, Andy was confined to his bed with round-the-clock help.

During the last year of Andy's life, Joel visited every day. In his memoir *Let Me Finish*, Andy's stepson, Roger Angell, writes:

> Joe told me that in that long year he'd read aloud to his father often, and discovered that he enjoyed listening to his own writings, though he wasn't always clear about who the author was. Sometimes he'd raise a hand and impatiently wave a passage away: not good enough. Other evenings, he'd listen to the end, almost at rest, and then ask again who'd written these words.
> "You did, Dad," Joe said.
> There was a pause, and Andy said, "Well, not bad."

Indeed, E. B. White's writing is, as they say in Maine, the finest kind.

While visiting the White farm on August 18, 1976, in North Brooklin, Maine, Jill Krementz took this photo of E. B. White on his rope swing—the same swing he describes in Charlotte's Web.

SENTENCES WE HATED TO COME TO THE END OF

All that I hope to say in books, all that I ever
hope to say, is that I love the world. I guess
you can find that in there, if you dig around.

E.B. WHITE DIED on October 1, 1985, at the age of eighty-six. He left instructions for his home to be sold; he did not want his farm turned into a museum. Ever since his childhood vow to "never to go up on a stage again," Andy had avoided public and private events: town meetings, weddings, graduations. So at his memorial service, Roger Angell reminded the congregation: "If Andy White could be with us today he would not be with us today."

His obituary in *The New Yorker* read, in part, "White had abundantly that most precious and least learnable of writerly gifts—the gift of inspiring affection in the reader." Whether he was working on a poem, a cartoon caption, an essay, or a children's book, E. B. White felt it was a writer's obligation "to transmit, as best he can, his love of life, his appreciation for the world." His friend and editor William Shawn said: "Even though White lived much of his life on a farm in Maine, remote from the clatter of publicity and celebrity, fame overtook him, fortunately leaving him untouched. His connections with nature were intimate and ardent. He loved his farm, his farm animals, his neighbors, his family and words."

E. B. White never believed that writers were celebrities. He wrote that when he was a child, an author "was a mythical being. . . . The book was the thing, not the man behind

October 1, 1985

the book." He did not seek literary approval and never considered himself a great reader—he preferred reading farm journals and boating magazines.

Much of what he wrote was not for children, yet many consider *Charlotte's Web* not only White's magnum opus but one of the best children's books ever written. Did E. B. White ever wish he'd written a masterpiece for adults? His stepson Roger Angell said the thought would not have occurred to him. Andy once said, "Anyone who writes *down* to children is simply wasting his time. You have to write up, not down. Children are demanding. They are the most attentive, curious, eager, observant, sensitive, quick, and generally congenial readers on earth. . . . Children are game for anything. I throw them hard words, and they backhand them over the net."

In his essays, White wrote about the environment, racism, world government, and other complex topics with a keen wit. He maintained he wrote "by ear" for an audience of one, and in reviewing *Essays of E. B. White*, Ben DeMott describes the sound of his words as "music": "The man knows all the tunes, all the limited lovely music that a plain English sentence can play." John Updike, who worked with Andy at *The New Yorker* (Katharine White was his editor) remembered "how much more *fun*" Andy seemed to have than the rest of the younger staff. "Not loud or obvious fun, but contained, inturning fun."

But there were a few critics along the way (and not just young readers wanting to know whether Stuart Little ever found Margalo; "I don't like the way it ends, it makes me sad," one young reader wrote). Criticism came in 1947 from the *New York Herald Tribune* during the McCarthy era when E. B. White fiercely opposed the blacklisting of Americans who refused to answer questions about their loyalty or political beliefs. White shot back to the newspaper editors: "I am a member of a party of one . . . I hold it that it would be improper for any committee or any employer to examine my conscience. . . . It is not a crime to believe anything at all in America." White believed profoundly in freedom: "To be free, in a planetary sense, is to feel you belong to the earth. To be free, in a social sense, is to feel at home in a democratic framework."

And to be free as a writer meant he was able to write as he pleased, to get down on paper a "little capsule of truth." That truth came out in simple, clear sentences, writing that William Shawn described as "utterly beautiful. . . . He was ageless, and his writing was timeless."

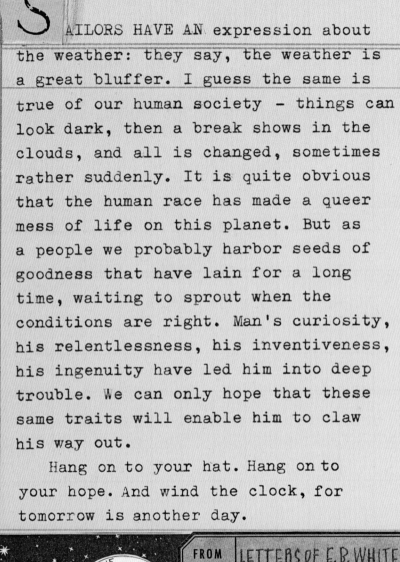

S AILORS HAVE AN expression about
the weather: they say, the weather is
a great bluffer. I guess the same is
true of our human society - things can
look dark, then a break shows in the
clouds, and all is changed, sometimes
rather suddenly. It is quite obvious
that the human race has made a queer
mess of life on this planet. But as
a people we probably harbor seeds of
goodness that have lain for a long
time, waiting to sprout when the
conditions are right. Man's curiosity,
his relentlessness, his inventiveness,
his ingenuity have led him into deep
trouble. We can only hope that these
same traits will enable him to claw
his way out.

Hang on to your hat. Hang on to
your hope. And wind the clock, for
tomorrow is another day.

FROM LETTERS OF E.B. WHITE

DATE 1973

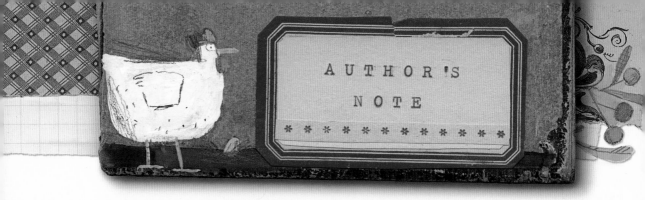

AUTHOR'S NOTE

* * * * * * * * * * * *

It has been ambitious and plucky of me to attempt to describe what is indescribable.... [But] a writer, like an acrobat, must occasionally try a stunt that is too much for him.

N O ONE COULD have prepared me for the sheer joy of diving into E. B. White's oeuvre. In reading his children's books, essays, and letters, I felt, as White wrote about his time in Maine, "as a child sees, feels, and listens."

When I read his introduction to *A Basic Chicken Guide for the Small Flock Owner*, I gained specific insight as to how to approach the book I was trying to create. White writes that he had been devoted to hens since 1907 and how as a boy he felt the "miracle of incubation" and "awe at an egg pipped from within after 21 days." He offers practical guidelines for would-be chicken owners: "Be tidy. Be brave. . . . Walk, don't run." And though his words pertain to chickens, I found them to be sound advice while writing this book: "There are moments and days of discouragement. . . . There are other moments and days which are richly rewarding and exhilarating."

In Maine, much of the landscape as E. B. White knew it is still there, arrested in time: canoes skim across lakes, sailboats cruise into harbors, long blue shadows appear on winter after-noons. All the minuscule details are here too: Moxie soda and tiny birchbark canoes are still for sale; *A. cavatica* can still be found in barn doorways.

For years, readers have wished they could see where E. B. White lived, to follow his footsteps in the "dung and the dark" of the barn. But he would discourage it. There's a saying in Maine: *You can't get there from here.* His granddaughter Martha White suggests that to get know her grandfather, to find his "boundless and gallant capacity for wonder," take a ride on a train, visit Belgrade Lakes, or sail or paddle in a boat of any size.

Even better, read anything he wrote: *It's all there if you dig around . . .*

Salutations,

Melissa Sweet

ABOUT
THE
ART

I SET OUT TO capture two things as I began the art for this book: the sense of place in White's writing and the small, vivid details he describes. In researching this book I visited Cornell University and saw the landscape of Ithaca. I traveled to New York City and to Maine's Belgrade Lakes and Blue Hill peninsula, drawing and photographing along the way.

White's barn (and the bits and pieces one might find in a barn in Maine) inspired my materials: snippets of wood, baling wire, screws, and nails and fastenings. A box of vintage office supplies— old paper clips, labels, and cellophane tape (which I imagined were akin to what might've been in stock at the *New Yorker* offices)— along with pieces of old books, handmade papers, watercolors, pencils, and a manual typewriter (to type White's quotes) provided a rich toolbox. Finally, because eggs, in all their guises, occur so often in his writing (in forewords, essays, and *Charlotte's Web*, of course), the front endpapers are a collage of White's writings about eggs, and both the back and front endpapers depict real goose eggs that were laid during the spring I began the art. As E. B. White wrote, "All beginnings are wonderful."

When melissa sweet approached me to say she had decided to write and illustrate a children's biography of E. B. White, I didn't hesitate to give her the White family's nod of approval. I knew her work from when my children were small, and I had always found it imaginative, quirky, and fun—plus, it was full of dogs. I had just finished editing a collection of my grandfather's writings about his various canine companions, *E. B. White on Dogs*, so that detail was important. That she and I are neighbors made it even more convenient, and we quickly fell into the habit of sharing photos and stories. Before long, Melissa showed up with a goose egg for me, its innards carefully blown out, and the shell beautifully adorned with a delicate copper wire and an E. B. White quotation on an illustrated tag: "I am sending you what I think is one of the most beautiful and miraculous things in the world—an egg." It was from a letter he had written to some sixth-graders in Los Angeles, in 1973. That egg was from one of his geese, Felicity, and he was sending it across the country as a thank-you for some essays the class had written. Melissa's egg was from

E. B. White with his dog Minnie in his New Yorker *office.*

another Maine farm, and it was an early signal that she was on the right track in her research on E. B. White.

I knew Melissa primarily as an illustrator, but I was familiar with some of the books she had written herself, as well. Children's books are even harder to write than other books, in my opinion, because children are very demanding about the sentences that draw their attention. There wasn't a needless word, as William Strunk, Jr. would have called it, in any of her books. But the clincher was that Melissa (and the author Jen Bryant) had just launched *The Right Word: Roget and His Thesaurus*. Peter Mark Roget was a man, like my grandfather, who cared deeply about choosing exactly the right word. When I saw that book, and how Melissa had chosen to illustrate Roget's word lists, I knew she had spent many months living inside of a thesaurus, and inside the mind of the man (and boy) who first created it. I own an old thesaurus, *Roget's International Thesaurus* from 1944, one of many books that migrated from my grandfather's bookshelves to mine. It is sun-bleached and tattered, dog-eared from use, and its spine is falling apart. I wouldn't replace it for the

E. B. White and Martha White at Allen Cove in Maine.

world. Like a favorite cookbook, it has been endlessly useful, lived in, and well loved, and it remains within easy reach. My grandfather once wrote about letters, "The visitor to the attic knows the risk he runs when he lifts the lid from a box of old letters. Words out of the past have the power to detain. Hours later he may find himself still crouched on the floor, savoring the pains and embarrassments of an early love, and with leg cramps to boot." ["Forward," July 30, 1932, *Points of My Compass*] It is the same with a thesaurus: you can get lost in it, and I'm sure my grandfather often did. Melissa Sweet could have had no better training.

The first time I toured Melissa's studio in Rockport, I had one of those rare moments of imagining a path not taken. Wouldn't it be fun to be Melissa Sweet? Her studio exudes creativity, curiosity, color, and light. The ground floor is well organized, like a library or archivist's office, and you want to open every drawer and peek inside. The upstairs is where the paint pots come out and ink might get spilled, but the effect is not messy or scattered. It is immediately clear that this is a place where a great talent is not just at work, but at play. Like my grandfather, Melissa Sweet has somehow kept that childlike sense of wonder at the world and (thankfully) found an avenue to share it with the rest of us. She is an observer, sometimes a collector, and she seems to work from a place of gratitude for the natural beauty that surrounds us— maybe especially here on the coast of Maine.

E. B. White with his dog Jones.

In her Author's Note, Melissa mentions a poultry primer and the introduction my grandfather had written, with his pithy advice, "Be tidy. Be brave." That book had passed from his bookshelves to mine when I started to keep a small flock of my own. He also advised, "Don't try to convey your enthusiasm for chickens to anyone else." That remains true about chickens, but I suspect it's not the case when it comes to favorite children's books, or their writers or illustrators. I hereby convey to you my unbridled enthusiasm for Melissa Sweet, and, assuming you have chosen to read this Johnny-come-lately Afterword, I offer you the White Literary LLC seal of approval on this Sweet biography. Consider

E. B. White and his dog Susy photographed by Jill Krementz on February 26, 1973, at his writing desk in Brooklin, Maine.

it authorized, because Melissa is clearly not just its author but an accurate authority on my grandfather.

When Scott Elledge completed his book *E. B. White: A Biography*, my grandfather sent him a thank-you note that ended with the lines, "I know how hard it is to write about a fellow who spends most of his time crouched over a typewriter. That was my fate, too." Melissa Sweet has faced the same challenge, plus that of translating his many years and extensive works into a children's biography. Through her great skill, care, and talent, she has brought it to life with color and humor and playfulness. Here, in these pages, you will find the grandfather I remember so well, the man with a dachshund on his desk and his hands on a manual typewriter. Now, thanks to Melissa Sweet, you can know him too.

White Literary LLC

Capital *E* begins
descending three-f
short turn to righ
top and uniting to
space, and joined by
to main slant, to a
Princi[

1899

1899: Elwyn Brooks White is born on July 11.
—The Croton Reservoir in New York City is demolished in order to construct the New York Public Library.

1902: Katharine Sergeant (age nine) wins a Silver Badge from *St. Nicholas* magazine for her essay "A Discovery," about a spider's nest.

1904: Edna St. Vincent Millay (age twelve) publishes a poem in *St. Nicholas* magazine.

—The White family spends the first of many Augusts in Belgrade Lakes, Maine.

1908: En publishes "A Story of a Mouse" in the *Woman's Home Companion*.

1910

1910: William Faulkner (age fourteen) publishes a drawing in *St. Nicholas* magazine.
—En's story "A Winter Walk" garners a Silver Badge from *St. Nicholas* magazine.

1911: The New York Public Library opens. The librarian Anne Carroll Moore later supervises the Children's Room. (By 1913, children's books account for one-third of all books withdrawn from the New York City branch libraries.)

1913: En garners a Gold Badge from *St. Nicholas* magazine for "A True Dog Story."

1914: World War I begins.

1917: En graduates from high school and later attends Cornell University in the fall. He enlists in the war effort as a farm cadet.

1918: Andy registers for the draft, but is declined because he doesn't weigh enough. He later enlists in the Student Army Training Corp at Cornell, but the war is over before he serves.
—The English professor Will Strunk, Jr. publishes *The Elements of Style* for his students at Cornell.

1919: World War I ends.

1920

1920: Eudora Welty (age ten) publishes a drawing in *St. Nicholas* magazine.

1921: Andy graduates from Cornell University.

1922: Andy buys a Model T Ford and makes a cross-country road trip with his Cornell classmate Howard Cushman, and later works for the *Seattle Times*.
—The Newbery Medal (named after the bookseller John Newbery) is established by Frederic G. Melcher, publisher, bookseller, and leader in library science. The medal is awarded annually for the most distinguished contribution to American literature for children.
—Rachel Carson (age fourteen) publishes her essay "My Favorite Recreation," about a day of bird watching, in *St. Nicholas* magazine.

1923: Andy travels to Alaska and Siberia on a cruise ship, working on the ship for his return passage.
—Andy returns home to New York.

1925: *The New Yorker* publishes its first issue on February 19. *The New Yorker* publishes a piece by E. B. White in April, and another in May.

1926: Andy begins working part-time at *The New Yorker*.
—While traveling by train in the Shenandoah Valley, he dreams of a dapper-dressed mouse. Notes from this dream would later become *Stuart Little*.

1927: Andy accepts a full-time position at *The New Yorker*.

1929: Andy marries Katharine Sergeant Angell on November 19.
—E. B. White publishes his first book, THE LADY IS COLD, a collection of poems.
—E. B. White and James Thurber co-author IS SEX NECESSARY?, a parody on relationships.

1930

1930: Andy and Katharine's son, Joel McCoun White, is born on December 21.

1931: E. B. White publishes HO-HUM: NEWSBREAKS FROM THE NEW YORKER, a collection of Newbreaks illustrated by Otto Soglow. ("Ho" was a pen name used by Andy for collaborations with his friend Cush, who was "Hum.")

1932: E. B. White publishes ANOTHER HO-HUM: MORE NEWSBREAKS FROM THE NEW YORKER, a second collection of Newbreaks illustrated by Otto Soglow.

—Andy paints his only *New Yorker* cover.

1933: Katharine and Andy buy a saltwater farm on Allen Cove in Maine.

1934: E. B. White publishes EVERY DAY IS SATURDAY, a collection of *New Yorker* Notes and Comments.

1935: Andy's father, Samuel White, dies.

1936: Andy's mother, Jessie White, dies.
—E. B. White publishes FAREWELL TO THE MODEL T, a collection of two essays, one a tribute to the Model T and the other to traveling the back roads of America.

1937: Andy spends the year in Maine to write. Later in the year, Andy, Katharine, and Joel move to Maine.
—E. B. White begins writing the column "One Man's Meat" for *Harper's* magazine.

1937: The Caldecott Medal, named after the illustrator Randolph Caldecott, is established by Frederic G. Melcher, awarded annually to the artist for the most distinguished picture book for children.

1938: E. B. White publishes THE FOX OF PEAPACK AND OTHER POEMS, a collection of previously published poems.

1939: E. B. White publishes QUO VADIMUS: OR, THE CASE FOR THE BICYCLE, a collection of humorous sketches.
—World War II begins.

1940

1941: E. B. White and Katharine White co-edit A SUBTREASURY OF AMERICAN HUMOR, a collection of works by their favorite humorists, including Don Marquis, Mark Twain, and Dorothy Parker.

1942: E. B. White publishes ONE MAN'S MEAT, a collection of his essays for *Harper's* magazine.

1943: The Whites return to New York City to live and continue their jobs at *The New Yorker*. Joel attends boarding school.
—The final issue of *St. Nicholas* magazine is published.

1945: E. B. White publishes STUART LITTLE.
—*The New Yorker* sends White as a correspondent to San Francisco to report on a conference discussing the formation of the United Nations.
—World War II ends.

1946: E. B. White publishes THE WILD FLAG, editorials first published in *The New Yorker* that commented on the idea of a world government. He later wrote his brother Stan that this book will establish him as a "THINKER."

1948: Fred, the family dachshund, dies.
—E. B. White is awarded honorary degrees from Dartmouth College, the University of Maine, and Yale University.

1949: E. B. White publishes "Here Is New York," an essay about strolling around Manhattan, written one sweltering summer from a hotel room in New York City.

1950

1950: E. B. White is awarded an honorary degree from Bowdoin College.
—E. B. White writes the foreword for *The Best of Archy and Mehitabel* by Don Marquis.

1951: Harold Ross dies.

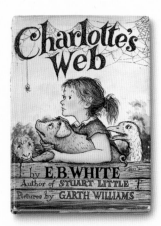

1952: E. B. White publishes CHARLOTTE'S WEB.
—E. B. White is awarded an honorary degree from Hamilton College.

1953: E. B. White is awarded a Newbery Honor for *Charlotte's Web*.
—E. B. White receives honorary degrees from Harvard University and Colby College.

1954: E. B. White publishes `THE SECOND TREE FROM THE CORNER`, stories, poems, and essays that originally appeared in *The New Yorker*.

1957: The Whites move permanently back to their farm in Maine.

1958: Rachel Carson asks E. B. White to write about the danger of pesticides on the environment. White urges Carson to write about it for *The New Yorker*. Her articles for the magazine would later become her book *Silent Spring*.

1959: `THE ELEMENTS OF STYLE` by Strunk and White is published.

1960

1960: E. B. White receives a Gold Medal for Essays and Criticisms from the National Institute of Letters.

1961: James Thurber dies.

1962: E. B. White publishes `THE POINTS OF MY COMPASS`, a chronological collection of essays and "Letters" from the *The New Yorker*. In response to *The New Yorker's* "Letters'" from far-flung correspondents (and since White "seldom went anywhere"), he created a new "compass" using his

New Yorker office on Forty-Third Street as his locus. From this vantage point, anything he wrote was a "letter from the East, North, South, or West."

1963: E. B. White is awarded the Presidential Medal of Freedom by President John F. Kennedy. He decides to attend this ceremony, but in the meantime, President Kennedy is assassinated. He writes Kennedy's obituary for *The New Yorker*.

1964: The Maine senator Edmund Muskie presents E. B. White the Presidential Medal of Freedom.

1970

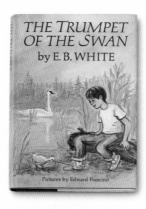

1970: E. B. White publishes `THE TRUMPET OF THE SWAN`.

—He receives the Laura Ingalls Wilder Award, honoring an author or illustrator whose books have made a lasting contribution to literature for children.

1971: E. B. White is awarded the National Medal for Literature.

1973: E. B. White is elected to the American Academy of Arts and Letters.

1976: E. B. White publishes `LETTERS OF E. B. WHITE`, an edited collection of letters written over his lifetime.

1977: Katharine Sergeant White dies after a series of long illnesses.
—E. B. White publishes `ESSAYS OF E. B. WHITE`, a collection of previously published essays.
—E. B. White edits and writes the foreword to Katharine's only book, *Onward and Upward in the Garden*, a collection of essays and journals originally published in *The New Yorker*.

1978: E. B. White is awarded a Pulitzer Prize special citation for letters.

1980

1981: E. B. White publishes `POEMS AND SKETCHES OF E. B. WHITE`, a collection of works spanning his entire career.

1982: E. B. White resigns from *The New Yorker*.

1985: E. B. White dies at his home on October 1.

NOTES

In the notes, sources frequently cited are identified by the following abbreviations:

EBW: E. B. White
KSW: Katharine Sergeant White

ix *"I believed then"*: EBW, "The Egg Is All," *New York Times.*

All's Right with the World Department

"All's Right": EBW, New Yorker Newsbreak Department Heads, White Literary LLC archive.

1   *"I fell in love"*: Ibid. EBW, "The Egg Is All," *New York Times.*

"square in the eyes": EBW to Stanley White, January 1927, *Letters*, 264.

"This is where": Ibid. Italics mine.

4   *"For six years"*: EBW, "Dog Training," *One Man's Meat*, 163.

5   *"As a child"*: Plimpton and Crowther, "The Art of the Essay."

6   *"One of the fringe benefits"*: EBW, *Letters*, 3.

7   *"Oh, the joy, the joy"*: Elledge, *E. B. White*, 11.

"Elwyn, my dear boy": Ibid., 4–5.

Once More to the Lake

"Once More to the Lake": EBW, "Once More to the Lake," *One Man's Meat*, 198.

9   *"Life is always a rich"*: EBW, *Charlotte's Web*, 176.

10 *"We Whites were"*: EBW, *Letters*, 8.

"summer without end": EBW, "Once More to the Lake," *One Man's Meat*, 201.

"like barn swallows in their nest": EBW, *Letters*, 9.

11 *"It was just a cheap"*: EBW, *Trumpet of the Swan*, 5.

"I wonder what": Ibid., 34.

12 *"the stillness of the cathedral"*: EBW, "Once More to the Lake," *One Man's Meat*, 199.

13 *"There was a lake"*: EBW, "A Boy I Knew," 34.

14 *"one of the most beautiful"*: EBW, "Belgrade Lake and Snug Harbor Camps."

17 *"The month of August"*: EBW, *Letters*, 7.

Years of Wonder

"Years of Wonder": EBW, "The Years of Wonder," *The Points of My Compass*, 205.

19 *"I took to writing early"*: EBW, *Letters*, 1.

20 *"A Story of a Little Mouse"*: EBW, "A Story of a Little Mouse."

"I wrote a poem": EBW, Elledge, *E. B. White*, 9.

21 *"an industrious"*: EBW, "St. Nicholas League," *Essays of E. B. White*, 281.

   "pigeons, dogs, snakes,": EBW, "About a Boy," *Readers Digest*, 35.

22 *"A True Dog Story"*: EBW, *St. Nicholas*, 1045.

23 *"was getting to and fro"*: Elledge, *E. B. White*, 33.

   "I don't know": EBW, "First World War," *One Man's Meat*, 88.

   "My utter dependence galls me": Ibid.

   "Eighteen and still no future": Ibid.

24 *"I didn't care for athletics"*: EBW, *Letters*, 10.

26 *"omit needless words"*: Elledge, *E. B. White*, 49.

   "This morning came news": EBW, to Jessie Hart White, December 1918, *Letters*, 19.

27 *"I'd send my son"*: Elledge, *E. B. White*, 49.

   "a memorable man": Strunk and White, *Elements of Style*, viii.

28 *"transported"*: EBW, Memorial Day Speech.

   "A matter of garb": Bainton, *George Lincoln Burr*, 135, 137.

   "was the single greatest": EBW, Memorial Day Speech.

   "with blinding clarity": Ibid.

29 *"To be free"*: EBW, "Freedom," *One Man's Meat*, 138.

   4 From Sea to Shining Sea

30 *"A person who"*: EBW, *Stuart Little*, 131.

   "true destination was": *Farewell to Model T*, 31.

31 *"travelling light"*: EBW, "A Slight Sound at Evening," *Essays of E. B. White*, 293.

   "The Model T": EBW, *Farewell to Model T*, 29–30, 34.

32 *"A young man who liked"*: EBW, *Writings from "The New Yorker,"* 227.

33 *"Now, if ever"*: EBW to Pete Vischer, April 1922, *Letters*, 37.

34 *"That afternoon we"*: EBW to Samuel and Jessie White, June 27, 1922, *Letters*, 47.

35 *"never make a good"*: LaBrie, *E. B. White*, 33.

   "a track across": EBW, *Farewell to the Model T; From Sea to Shining Sea*, 30.

   "Just say the words": EBW, "Time Past, Time Future," *Second Tree from the Corner*, 12.

36 *"sheer glory"*: EBW, "Notes and Comments," *The New Yorker*, 1960, 31.

   "sails made of bed sheets": Ibid., 101.

   "swung into Grand Central Terminal": Ibid., 102.

   5 Answers to Hard Questions

   "Answers to Hard Questions": EBW, New Yorker Newsbreak Department Heads, White Literary LLC archive.

37 *"I discovered"*: EBW to Stanley White, January 1929, *Letters*, 82.

   "short writer": Ibid., 70.

   "short, relaxed, and sometimes funny": Ibid.

37 *"a moment in the sun"*: EBW, "Notes and Comments," *The New Yorker*, 31.

38 *"the gift of loneliness"*: EBW, *Here Is New York*, 19.

   "FOR THINGS THAT": EBW, "For Things That Are a Part of Me," *The Conning Tower*.

39 *"Dear Mr. White"*: KSW to EBW, in collection of Martha White.

41 *"two desks, two"*: EBW, *Letters*, 71.

   "From the start": Elledge, *E. B. White*, 132.

42 *"slip moodily out"*: Thurber, EBW," *Credos and Curios*, 134.

43 *"Thurber wrote the way"*: EBW, "James Thurber," 247.

   "No one can write a sentence": LaBrie, *E. B. White*, 40.

   "He made me": Kunkel, *Genius in Disguise*, 149.

   "One of the persons": Elledge, *E. B. White*, 130.

44 *"There is a secret"*: EBW, *Ho Hum*, vii.

46 *"It was a very nice wedding"*: *E. B. White on Dogs*, xi.

47 *"irreplaceable"*: Yagoda, *About Town*, 79.

   "I sat there": EBW, *Letters*, 70.

   "Natural History": EBW to KSW, November 30, 1929, *Letters*, 88.

48 *"E.B. White slowly accustomed"*: EBW, interoffice memo cartoon to KSW, November 1929, *Letters*, 87.

   "What [White] feels": EBW to KSW, Spring 1930, *Letters*, 89.

49 *"Some day when"*: EBW, "Apostrophe to a Pram Rider," *The Conning Tower*, 1931.

50 *"To a writer"*: EBW to Gustave S. Lobrano, December 1930, *Letters*, 97.

53 *"What happens to"*: EBW, *Points of My Compass*, 30.

   6 A Time of Enchantment

   "A Time of Enchantment": EBW, *One Man's Meat*, xiii.

54 *"When I got a place"*: EBW, *Charlotte's Web* publicity quote for Harper and Brothers, White Collection.

   "The hope I see": EBW, "Alice Through the Cellophane."

55 *"My Year"*: EBW, *Letters*, 145.

   "The best writing": EBW, "Questionnaire," *One Man's Meat*, 234.

56 *"school-in-country"*: EBW, "Education," *One Man's Meat*, 44.

   "just like lightning": Ibid.

   "E. B. White purchased": Martha White, *E. B. White on Dogs*, 62.

57 *"I have discovered"*: EBW to John R. Fleming, September 15, 1945, *Letters*, 254.

58 *"The scow was"*: EBW to Jon Wilson, October 11, 1983, *Letters*, 669.

59 *"It must be"*: EBW, "Children's Books," *One Man's Meat*, 20.

   "with a passionate interest": EBW, "Coon Tree," *Essays of E. B. White*, 42.

   "dull": EBW, "Children's Books," *One Man's Meat*, 23.

"true spirit": Ibid., 23.

60 *"I feel sure you"*: Anne Carroll Moore to EBW, January 16, 1939, White Collection.

"I have a children's": EBW to James Thurber, April 16, [1938?], *Letters*, 164.

"would seem to": EBW to Eugene Saxton, March 1, [1939], *Letters*, 182.

"You will be shocked": Ibid.

62 *"Once in everyone's"*: EBW, Introduction to *One Man's Meat*, xiii.

(7) Stuart Little

64 *"My innocent tale"*: EBW, *New York Times*, March 6, 1966.

"I would rather": EBW to Eugene Saxton, April 11, 1939, *Letters*, 184.

65 *"a kite caught"*: Elledge, *E. B. White*, 251.

"I was almost sure": EBW, "The Librarian Said."

"Only another children's book editor": Nordstrom, "Stuart, Wilbur, Charlotte."

67 *"Schooner"*: EBW, Garth Williams Estate, Courtesy of Heritage Auctions.

68 *"I think Garth"*: EBW, unpublished letter, October 10, 1945, in Neumeyer, *The Annotated Charlotte's Web*, 198.

"Stuart Little is small": Advertising/Marketing Department, Harper and Brothers, White Collection.

"I was never": Sayers, *Anne Carroll Moore*, 242.

"monstrous birth": Silvey, *Children's Books*, 677.

"out of hand": Sayers, *Anne Carroll Moore*, 244.

"The two worlds are all": Ibid.

*"I fear **Stuart Little**"*: Ibid.

69 *"You are right"*: KSW to Anne Carroll Moore, *Letters*, 252.

70 *"Saw your book"*: EBW, "The Librarian Said."

"Not recommended for purchase": Lepore, *Mansion of Happiness*, 55.

71 *"Dear Mr. White"*: Clifton School students to EBW, March 11, 1946, White Collection.

72 *"In the loveliest town"*: EBW, *Stuart Little*, 100.

73 *"Have you any"*: EBW, *Stuart Little*, 102.

74 *"It is unnerving to be told"*: EBW, "The Librarian Said."

75 *"Dear Miss Nordstrom"*: EBW to Ursula Nordstrom, December 17, 1947, White Collection.

(8) Bad News

"Bad News": EBW, *Charlotte's Web*, 48.

77 *"A pig shall"*: EBW, Harper and Brothers publicity information, 1952, White Collection.

"vile": EBW, "Death of a pig."

"In no time at all": Ibid., 100.

"His activities and his character": EBW, "A Week in November," *One Man's Meat*, 264.

78 *"When a pig"*: EBW, "Death of a Pig."

78 *"I do not like to"*: Harper and Brothers publicity information, 1952, White Collection.

"double-dealing": Ibid.

"Fred is a notorious": EBW, "Death of a Pig."

79 *"I knelt, saw"*: Ibid.

80 *"supervising"*: Ibid.

"Fred patrolled": Ibid.

"The grave in the woods": Ibid.

81 *"[Fred's] grave is"*: EBW, "Bedfellows," *Essays of E. B. White*, 110–11.

Charlotte's Web

82 *"I had as much trouble"*: EBW, *The Annotated Charlotte's Web*, 1.

"a plain grey spider": Comstock, *Spider Book*, 472.

84 *"My next book is in sight"*: EBW to Cass Canfield, [October 19, 1949], *Letters*, 288.

"In this . . . I found": EBW to Gene Deitch, January 12, [1971], *Letters*, 563.

"some dancer": EBW, *Charlotte's Web*, Elledge, *E. B. White*, 294.

85 *"Wish you could"*: EBW to Ursula Nordstrom, March 27, 1952, *Letters*, 324.

86 *"ripen"*: EBW to Ursula Nordstrom, March 2, 1951, *Letters*, 303.

"Charlotte was a": EBW, White Collection.

92 *"just perfect"*: Garth Williams to Peter Neumeyer, *The Annotated Charlotte's Web*, 200.

"beguiling": EBW to Cass Canfield, March 29, 1952, *Letters*, 325.

"a New Englander": EBW to Gene Deitch, January 12, [1971], *Letters*, 562

"gruesome": Garth Williams to Peter Neumeyer, *The Annotated Charlotte's Web*, 200.

93 *"There is a"*: EBW to Ursula Nordstrom, March 28, 1952, *Letters*, 325.

94 *"White accepted the"*: Garth Williams to Peter Neumeyer, *The Annotated Charlotte's Web*, 200.

95 *"I struggled to invent"*: Ibid.

96 *"Why did you do"*: EBW, *Charlotte's Web*, 164.

98 *"What the book is"*: Welty, "Life in the Barn Was Very Good."

"the film should": EBW to Gene Deitch, January 12, [1971], *Letters*, 562.

"Templeton starts as": Ibid.

"It's ridiculous": EBW to Joe Berk, producer in an NPR interview, in Block, "Charlotte A. Cavatica."

99 *"I just want to add"*: EBW to Gene Deitch, January 12, [1971], *Letters*, 563.

The Elements of Style

100 *"A misspelled word"*: EBW, *Stuart Little*, 90.

"Walden is the only": EBW, "Visitors to the Pond," *Writings from the New Yorker*, 1925–1976, 44–45.

"simplicity, simplicity, simplicity": Thoreau, *Walden*, 57.

"the insistence": EBW, "A Slight Sound at Evening," *Essays of E. B. White*, 299.

101 *"little book"*: Strunk and White, *Elements of Style,* vii.

"clear, brief, bold": EBW, Ibid., xi.

102 *"Vigorous writing is"*: Ibid., ix.

"There you have a short": Ibid., ix.

103 *"Form the possessive"*: Strunk and White, *Elements of Style,* 1.

"Writing, to be effective": Ibid., 10.

"Exclamations": Ibid., 28.

"Like. Not to be": Ibid., 41.

"The approach to style": Ibid., 55.

104 *"White's points"*: Joyce Sidman interview, September 4, 2014.

"That. Which": Ibid., 47.

105 *"Bat Wraps Up"*: Sidman, *Dark Emperor,* 26.

106 *"[I have this rule] carved"*: Paul Fleischman interview, August 8 and September 4, 2014.

"Avoid the use": Strunk and White, *Elements of Style,* 59.

"I actually once tried": Paul Fleischman interview, August 8 and September 4, 2014.

107 *"Though I have"*: Kate DiCamillo interview, August 25, 2014.

"revising is part": Strunk and White, *Elements of Style,* 58.

"Do not be afraid": Ibid., 58.

108 *"When I finally"*: EBW to Davis Dodd, October 27, [1971], *Letters,* 576–77.

"I feel a terrible": EBW to Jack Case, December 17, 1958, *Letters,* 416.

"Dear Jack": EBW to Jack Case, March 30, [1962], *Letters,* 447.

11 The Trumpet of the Swan

109 *"In almost everyone's life"*: EBW, *Trumpet of the Swan,* 174.

"Probably in a sock somewhere": EBW, *Letters,* 324.

110 *"needed money"*: EBW to young reader, March 9, 1973, *Letters,* 593.

"Dear Cush": EBW to Howard Cushman, October 10, 1968, *Letters,* 515–16.

"I've never visited": Ibid.

112 *"The snapshots from"*: EBW to Howard Cushman, [November? 1968], *Letters,* 520.

"Dear Ursula": EBW to Ursula Nordstrom, November 17, 1969, *Letters,* 536.

113 *"I'm very sad tonight"*: EBW to Garth Williams, December 31, 1969, *Letters,* 541.

114 *"The day Sam Beaver"*: EBW, *Trumpet of the Swan,* 174–75.

115 *"The sky is"*: Ibid., 172.

116 *"I go by my instinct"*: EBW to young readers, March 9, 1973, *Letters,* 593.

"Father was quite": Elledge, *E. B. White,* 10.

117 *"Welcome to the pond"*: EBW, *Trumpet of the Swan,* 30–31.

118 *"The world of E. B. White's"*: Updike, *New York Times,* June 28, 1970.

118 *"Imagine me . . . sitting"*: EBW to Reginald Allen, January 2, 1971, *Letters*, 561.

119 *"Sam Beaver's poem"*: EBW, *Trumpet of the Swan*, 181–82.

(12)   What Do Our Hearts Treasure?

"What Do Our Hearts Treasure": EBW, "What Do Our Hearts Treasure," *Essays of E. B. White*, 189.

120 *"Old age is a special"*: Shenker, "E. B. White."

"When I want": EBW to Mary Virginia Parrish, *Letters*, 532.

122 *"launched a thousand"*: EBW, Interview with Martha White, April 2013.

"I have lost the one": Elledge, *E. B. White*, 354.

"The trip was a success": EBW to Scott Elledge, *Letters*, August 25, 1982, 655.

124 *"The year is only"*: EBW to Dr. and Mrs. Ray Conover, [January 1984], *Letters*, 673.

125 *"I'll be 85 in July"*: EBW to Miles Katzenstein, [circa May 1, 1984], *Letters*, 681.

126 *"gainfully employed"*: EBW to William Shawn, April 26, [1982], *Letters*, 646.

"Joe told me": Angell, *Let Me Finish*, 137.

(13)   Sentences We Hated to Come to the End Of

"Sentences We Hated To": EBW, New Yorker Newsbreak Department Heads, White Literary LLC archive.

128 *"All that I hope to"*: Elledge, *E. B. White*, 300-01.

"If Andy White": Angell, *Let Me Finish*, 119.

129 *"White had abundantly"*: Angell, Shawn, and Updike, "Notes and Comment."

"to transmit as best": EBW, unpublished letter in response to the Laura Ingalls Wilder Award, 1970, White Literary LLC archive.

"Even though White": Mitgang, "EB White, Essayist and Stylist Dies"

"was a mythical being": EBW to Miss B—, May 7, 1961, *Letters*, 438.

130 *"Anyone who writes down"*: Plimpton and Crowther, "The Art of the Essay."

"by ear": Root, *E. B. White*, 181.

"music. The man": Root, *E. B. White*, 221.

*"how much more **fun**"*: Updike, *Picked-Up Pieces*, 417.

131 *"Not loud"*: Ibid.

"I don't like the way": Letter to E. B. White, White Collection.

"I am a member of a party": EBW to the *New York Herald Tribune*, November 29, 1947, *Letters*, 267–68.

"To be free, in a planetary sense": EBW, "Freedom," *One Man's Meat*, 138.

"little capsule of truth": EBW to Stanley White, [January 1929], *Letters*, 82.

"utterly beautiful": Mitgang, "E. B. White."

132 *"Sailors have an expression"*: EBW to Mr. Nadeau, March 30, 1973, *Letters*, 596.

Author's Note

134 ***"It has been"***: EBW, "Ring of Time," *Essays of E. B. White*, 182.

"*as a child*": EBW, *One Man's Meat*, xiii.

"miracle of incubation": Jones, *A Basic Chicken Guide*, viii.

"awe at an egg": Ibid.

"*Be tidy*": Ibid., vi.

"There are moments": Ibid., viii.

"dung and the dark": EBW, *Charlotte's Web*, 164.

135 ***"boundless and gallant"***: Angell, Shawn, and Updike, "Notes and Comment."

About the Art

135 "All beginnings": EBW, "Danbury Fair," *The New Yorker*, October 18, 1930, 20.

Timeline

142 ***"Thinker"***: EBW, *Letters*, 260.

143 ***"seldom went anywhere"***: EBW, *Points of My Compass*, xii.

Thank-Yous

157 "You have been": EBW, *Charlotte's Web*, 164.

"terrific, terrific, terrific": Ibid., 88.

"Thank you": Ibid., 170.

158 "not proud": Ibid., 140.

162 ***"Dear Sixth Graders"***: EBW to "Some Sixth Graders in Los Angeles," May 20, 1973, *Letters*, 596–97.

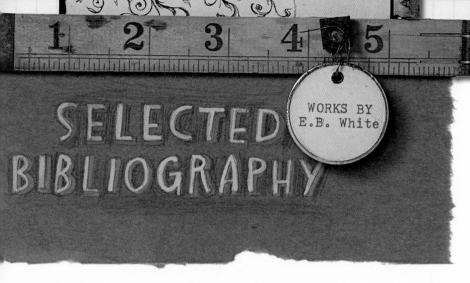

"Alice Through the Cellophane." *The New Yorker,* May 20, 1933.

The Annotated Charlotte's Web. Introduction and notes by Peter F. Neumeyer. New York: HarperCollins, 1994.

"Belgrade Lake and Snug Harbor Camps." Handwritten brochure, 1914. Collection of Martha White.

"A Boy I Knew." *Reader's Digest,* June 1940, 33–36.

Charlotte's Web. New York: Harper and Brothers, 1952.

"Cross-Word Enigma." *St. Nicholas,* October 1911, 1151.

"Death of a Pig." *Atlantic Monthly,* January 1948.

E. B. White on Dogs. Edited by Martha White. Gardiner, ME: Tilbury House, 2013.

"The Egg Is All." Remarks on receiving the National Medal for Literature. Reprinted in the *New York Times,* December 7, 1971.

Essays of E. B. White. New York: HarperCollins, 1992.

Every Day Is Saturday. New York: Harper and Brothers, 1934.

Farewell to Model T; From Sea to Shining Sea, with Lee Strout White [Richard Lee Strout]. New York: Little Book Room, 2003. First published 1936 by Putnam's.

The Fox of Peapack and Other Poems. New York: Harper and Brothers, 1938.

Here Is New York. Introduction by Roger Angell. New York: Little Book Room, 1999.

Ho Hum: Newsbreaks from the "New Yorker." New York: Farrar and Rinehart, 1931.

In the Words of E. B. White. Edited by Martha White. Ithaca, NY: Cornell University Press, 2011.

"James Thurber." *The New Yorker,* November 11, 1961, 247.

The Letters of E. B. White. Edited by Martha White. Rev. ed. New York: HarperCollins, 2006.

"The Librarian Said It Was Bad for Children." *New York Times,* March 6, 1966.

Memorial Day Speech. May 1940. White Collection.

One Man's Meat. Thomaston, ME: Tilbury House, 1997.

Poems and Sketches of E. B. White. New York: Harper and Row, 1983.

The Points of My Compass. New York: Harper and Row, 1962.

Quo Vadimus? Or the Case for the Bicycle. New York: Grosset and Dunlap, 1938.

The Second Tree from the Corner. New York: HarperCollins, 1989. First published 1954 by Harper and Row.

"A Story of a Little Mouse." Letter to Albert White, October 21, 1908, White Collection.

Stuart Little. New York: HarperCollins, 1973. First published 1945 by Harper and Brothers.

A Subtreasury of American Humor. Edited by E. B. White and Katharine White. New York: Random House, 1948.

"A True Dog Story." *St. Nicholas,* 41, no. 11 (September 1914): 1045.

The Trumpet of the Swan. New York: Harper and Row, 1970.

"What Am I Saying to My Readers?" *New York Times,* May 14, 1961.

White Collection. Division of Rare and Manuscript Collections, Cornell University Library, Ithaca, New York.

The Wild Flag. Boston: Houghton Mifflin, 1946.

Writings from "The New Yorker." Edited by Rebecca Dale. New York: HarperCollins, 2006.

Angell, Roger. *Let Me Finish.* New York: Harcourt, 2006.

Angell, Roger, William Shawn, and John Updike. "Notes and Comment." *The New Yorker,* October 14, 1985, 31–33.

Bainton, Roland H. *George Lincoln Burr: His Life.* Ithaca, NY: Cornell University Press, 1943.

Beard, Daniel C. *The American Boy's Handy Book.* New York: Charles Scribner's Sons, 1890.

Block, Melissa. "Charlotte A. Cavatica: Bloodthirsty, Wise and True." *All Things Considered.* National Public Radio, August 4, 2008.

Comstock, John Henry. *The Spider Book.* New York: Doubleday, 1912.

Elledge, Scott. *E. B. White: A Biography.* New York: W. W. Norton, 1985.

Fleischman, Paul. *Seedfolks.* New York: HarperCollins, 1997.

Garvey, Mark. *Stylized: A Slightly Obsessive History of Strunk and White's "The Elements of Style."* New York: Simon and Schuster, 2009.

Gertsch, Willis J. *American Spiders.* Princeton, NJ: D. Van Nostrand, 1949.

Gherman, Beverly. *E. B. White: Some Writer!* New York: Atheneum, 1992.

Gill, Brendan. *Here at the "New Yorker."* New York: Random House, 1975.

Hall, Katherine Romans. *E. B. White: A Bibliographic Catalogue of Printed Materials in the Department of Rare Books, Cornell University Library.* New York: Garland, 1979.

Jones, Roy F. *A Basic Chicken Guide for the Small Flock Owner.* Introduction by E. B. White. New York: William Morrow, 1944.

Kunkel, Thomas. *Genius in Disguise.* New York: Carroll and Graf, 1995.

Lepore, Jill. "The Lion and the Mouse." *New Yorker,* July 21, 2008.

———. *The Mansion of Happiness.* New York: Random House, 2012.

Long, William J. *A Little Brother to the Bear.* Boston: Athenaeum, 1903.

Marcus, Leonard. *Dear Genius: The Letters of Ursula Nordstrom.* New York: HarperCollins, 1998.

Marquis, Don. *The Lives and Times of Archy and Mehitabel.* Introduction by E. B. White. Garden City, NY: Doubleday, 1933.

Mitgang, Herbert. "E. B. White, Essayist and Stylist, Dies." *New York Times,* October 2, 1985.

LaBrie, Aimee. *E. B. White.* Who Wrote That? series. Philadelphia: Chelsea House, 2005.

The New Yorker Twenty-Fifth Anniversary Album, 1925–1950. New York: Harper and Brothers, 1951.

Nordstrom, Ursula. "Stuart, Wilbur, Charlotte: A Tale of Tales." *New York Times,* May 12, 1974.

Plimpton, George, and Frank H. Crowther. "The Art of the Essay, No. 1." *Paris Review* 48 (Fall 1969).

Robertson, Nan. "Life Without Katharine: E. B. White and His Sense of Loss." *New York Times,* April 8, 1980.

Root, Robert L. *E. B. White: The Emergence of an Essayist.* Iowa City: University of Iowa Press, 1999.

Sampson, Edward C. *E. B. White.* New York: Twayne, 1974.

Sayers, Frances Clarke. *Anne Carroll Moore.* New York: Scribner's, 1972.

Shenker, Israel. "E. B. White: Notes and Comment by Author." *New York Times,* July 11, 1969.

Silvey, Anita, ed. *Children's Books and Their Creators.* Boston: Houghton Mifflin, 1995.

Sidman, Joyce. *The Dark Emperor and other Poem of the Night,* Boston: Houghton Mifflin Harcourt, 2010.

Sims, Michael. *The Story of "Charlotte's Web."* New York: Walker, 2012.

Strunk, William, Jr., and E. B. White. *The Elements of Style.* New York: Macmillan, 1959.

Thoreau, Henry David. *Walden.* 1854. Radford, VA: Wilder, 2008.

Thurber, James. *Credos and Curios.* New York: Harper and Row, 1932

———. *The Years with Ross.* New York: HarperCollins, 2001.

Thurber, James, and E. B. White. *Is Sex Necessary?* New York: Harper Collins Publishers, 2004.

Tingum, Janice. *E. B. White: The Elements of a Writer.* Minneapolis: Lerner, 1995.

Updike, John. "Magnum Opus." *New Yorker,* July 12, 1999.

———. *Picked-Up Pieces.* New York: Random House, 2012.

Welty, Eudora. "Life in the Barn Was Very Good." *New York Times Book Review,* October 19, 1952.

———. *The Eye of the Storm: Selected Essays and Reviews.* New York: Random House, 1977.

Whynott, Douglas. *A Unit of Water, a Unit of Time: Joel White's Last Boat.* New York: Doubleday, 1999.

Yagoda, Ben. *About Town: The "New Yorker" and the World It Made.* New York: Scribner's, 2000.

AUDIO

Charlotte's Web. Read by the author. Listening Library, 2002. Audiobook CD, unabridged.

Stuart Little. Read by Julie Harris, Listening Library, 1999. Audiobook CD, unabridged.

The Trumpet of the Swan. Read by the author, Listening Library, 2006. Audiobook CD, unabridged.

The Trumpet of the Swan. Composed by Jason Robert Brown. Read by John Lithgow. P. S. Classics, 2011. Audio CD.

White on White. Read by Joel White. Blackstone Audio, 2008. Audio CD.

To read more about **James Thurber,** go to www.ThurberHouse.org.

THANK

YOUS

BECAUSE OF THE kindness and generosity of many people, this book became the one I envisioned. Great thanks go to the White family. I am especially indebted to Martha White for graciously sharing family photos, archival material, and stories. To my editor, Ann Rider, as Charlotte said so eloquently, "You have been my friend. . . . That in itself is a tremendous thing." My gratitude goes to everyone at Houghton Mifflin Harcourt, including Betsy Groban, publisher; Mary Wilcox, editor in chief; Sheila Smallwood, art director; Whitney Leader-Picone, senior designer; Ann-Marie Pucillo, managing editor; Alison Kerr Miller, manuscript editor; and Lily Kessinger, editorial assistant; and in production, Donna McCarthy and Trish McGinley. For being "terrific, terrific, terrific," designers Margo Halverson and Charles Melcher of Alice Design Communication, photographer Rick Kyle of 5000K Inc., and to the Cornell University Library, Division of Rare and Manuscript Collections, with special thanks to reference specialist Eisha Neely. For the benevolence and talent of my colleagues Kate DiCamillo, Paul Fleischman, Joyce Sidman, Harry Bliss, and my agent, Rebecca Sherman. For generously sharing their time and stories about Andy White: Anne Bray, Robert and Mary Gallant, and Dorothy Hayes. And to friends and family who cheered me on I turn to Wilbur's heartfelt words: "Thank you. . . . I will never forget this as long as I live."

While I was in the middle of making this book, my husband, Mark, decided to make me a replica of *Flounder* from the exact plans that E. B. White used in *The American Boy's Handy Book* (see page 58). I christened the scow *Wilbur*, because like the hero in *Charlotte's Web*, it is humble: "not proud and . . . near the ground." The thrill of watching this boat be built was second only to what I felt on its maiden voyage. Thank you with all my heart.

IMAGE CREDITS

INDEX

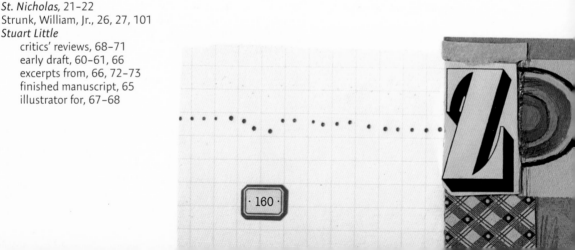

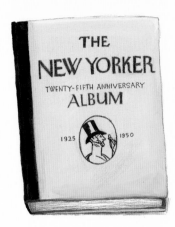

To my parents, who introduced me to E. B. White
by way of a book of New Yorker cartoons,
and to my brothers, who shared it with me.

All rights reserved. For information about permission to reproduce selections from this book, write to
trade.permissions@hmhco.com or to Permissions, Houghton Mifflin Harcourt Publishing Company,
3 Park Avenue, 19th Floor, New York, New York 10016.

hmhbooks.com

The illustrations for this book were done in watercolor, gouache, and mixed media,
using vintage ledger paper, and MacGregor Handmade Paper from Whiting, Maine.
The labels identifying E. B. White's quotes were letterpress printed by
The Ascensius Press in South Freeport, Maine.

The Library of Congress has cataloged the hardcover edition as follows:
Sweet, Melissa.
Some writer!: the story of E. B. White / by Melissa Sweet.
pages cm
1. White, E. B. (Elwyn Brooks), 1899–1985—Juvenile literature. 2. Authors, American—20th century—
Biography—Juvenile literature. 3. Children's stories—Authorship—Juvenile literature. I. Title.
PS3545.H5187Z926 2016
818'.5209—dc23
[B]   2015002079

ISBN: 978-0-544-31959-2 hardcover
ISBN: 978-0-358-13729-0 paperback

Manufactured in Malaysia
TWP 10 9 8 7 6 5 4 3 2 1
4500766243

DEAR SIXTH GRADERS:

Your essays spoke of beauty, of love, of light and darkness, of joy and sorrow, and of the goodness of life. They were wonderful compositions. I have seldom read any that have touched me more.

To thank you and your teacher Mrs. Ellis, I am sending you what I think is one of the most beautiful and miraculous things in the world—an egg. I have a goose named Felicity and she lays about forty eggs every spring. It takes her almost three months to accomplish this. Each egg is a perfect thing. I am mailing you one of Felicity's eggs. The insides have been removed—blown out—so the egg should last forever, or almost forever. I hope you will enjoy seeing this great egg and loving it. Thank you for sending me your essays about being somebody. I was pleased that so many of you felt the beauty and goodness of the world. If we can feel that when we are young, then there is great hope for us when we grow older.

Sincerely,
E.B. White

FROM LETTERS OF E.B. WHITE
DATE 1973

More from MELISSA SWEET

Winner of the Sibert Medal,
for Distinguished Informational Book

Winner of the NCTE Orbis Pictus Award,
for Excellence in Nonfiction

An ALA Notable Book

Winner of the Flora Stieglitz Straus Award

Winner of the Cook Prize,
honoring STEM books for children

"[A] brilliant combination of collage, design, illustration and text." —*New York Times Book Review*

★ "This clever marriage of information and illustration soars high." —*Kirkus Reviews*, starred review

★ "A joyous piece of nonfiction that informs and delights in equal parts." —*Booklist*, starred review

★ "Sweet tells this slice of American history well, conveying both Sarg's enthusiasm and joy in his work as well as the drama and excitement of the parade. . . . This one should float off the shelves."
—*School Library Journal*, starred review

Winner of the IRA Children's Book Award

"As informative as it is empowering." —*Horn Book*

"An outstanding collective biography of women and girls who changed the world with their inventions." —*School Library Journal*

"This book is an inspired ode to women inventors."
—*Publishers Weekly*

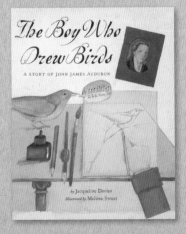

Selected for the Society of Illustrators' Show

A Junior Library Guild Selection

A New York Public Library Best Book

Winner of the Sigurd F. Olson Nature Writing Award

★ "Sweet's illustrations soar, incorporating mixed-media collage into her paintings in gloriously eclectic mélange that evokes both the time and Audubon's scientific enthusiasms."
—*Kirkus Reviews*, starred review